Dr. Del's Narrative Series:

Narratives of the Nativity of Jesus of Nazareth

Narratives of the Earthly Ministry of Jesus of Nazareth

Narratives of the Passion, Resurrection,
and Ascension of Jesus of Nazareth

Narratives of the Beginning of the Early Christian Church

Narratives of St. Paul's Missionary Journeys and Rome

NARRATIVES
OF ST. PAUL'S
MISSIONARY JOURNEYS
AND ROME

TOLD AS FIRST PERSON ACCOUNTS BY THE
MEN AND WOMEN WHO WITNESSED THEM

BOOK FIVE

Written by Del Mueller

Narrator illustrations by Allison Korenchan

authorHOUSE®

AuthorHouse™ LLC
1663 Liberty Drive
Bloomington, IN 47403
www.authorhouse.com
Phone: 1-800-839-8640

Published by AuthorHouse   07/29/2013

ISBN: 978-1-4772-6268-9 (sc)
ISBN: 978-1-4772-6269-6 (e)

Library of Congress Control Number: 2012916415

Dedicated to
a caring God
who guided this author
to craft realistic narratives
that offer a personal perspective to the
origin and growth of his New Testament Church

Acknowledgements

A project of this magnitude requires the care and attention beyond that of the author. To help bring this book to fruition I owe a special thanks to Dr. R. Allan Zimmer, Professor *emeritus*, Concordia University Chicago for his detailed editing of the manuscript. I am also blessed to have the participation of my wife, Dorleen, and retired educator and friend, Laura Latzke. Their careful examination of what I had written is sincerely appreciated.

Special thanks to Jeffery W. Hamilton, pastor of La Vista Church of Christ, La Vista, Nebraska, for his invaluable help securing many of the "intext" graphics used in this series.

Permission granted by the La Vista Church of Christ, La Vista, Nebraska for inclusion of the following graphics:
  Paul preached to the people
  Demetrius the silversmith
  Paul arrested during a riot in Jerusalem
  Paul shipwrecked
  Paul the author
  Paul arrives in Rome in chains

Note to the Reader

The story you are about to read is an historical novel based on chapters 13 through 28 of the *Acts of the Apostles*, a letter written by St. Luke to his friend Theophilis, and part of the New Testament Bible. *The Acts* is a continuation of St. Luke's first letter in which he detailed the earthly ministry of Christ.

Since it is generally agreed that Luke was not a participant of St. Paul's first missionary journey and part of the second journey [his first reference as a participant in *The Acts* is found in chapter 16:10], it can be assumed the content on which that earlier part of the book is based was the consequence of conversations Luke had with those who had personally witnessed these events. In chapter 16:10, Luke becomes part of the missionary group; identifying himself by using the pronoun "we" rather than the pronouns he used earlier, "they" and "them."

The narratives told in this book begin as Paul and Barnabas are called by the Holy Spirit to venture in what was then called Asia to witness Jesus as Messiah and risen Lord, and end with Paul's imprisonment in Rome under Caesar Nero.

✠ ✠ ✠

Each narrative is written as I envisioned the eye-witness could have told it. There is no certainty that my imaginations are correct; thus – a novel. The narratives are presented as *first-person* accounts of the events that took place during the spread of the Christian Church from Asia to Southern Europe; each told by a person who witnessed it.

I have attempted to posture *the reader* as the one who is listening to *the teller*; the person who lived the event. Therefore I entitled each narrative as: Then *The Teller* Said, and provided a brief biography and a graphic of that person.

I tried to tell the Biblical stories accurately; attempting to assure that nothing in the narratives conflicted directly with what is recorded in Holy Scriptures. However, to make a story line flow, it became necessary to provide anecdotal information when no detail was offered in the Scriptures. Where this happened, I invented actions, relationships, and dialogue that to me seemed possible and reasonable.

It may be assumed that some anecdotal narrative is poorly chosen and some imagined actions are not sufficiently supported by known facts. What is certain and faith building is not the peripheral information I have incorporated, but rather the teaching of Scripture alone.

A Bar Mitzvah kind of event is mentioned in the narratives. While there is no direct reference to it in Scripture, I assumed a similar rite of passage, which I labeled *Day of Dedication*, was practiced in the first century.

In the final narrative, *Then Paul Said*, the apostle tells of his travels following release from his first arrest, a house arrest in Rome; and following the burning of the capital city, his second imprisonment in Rome during a Nero promoted persecution of Christians. The content of this narrative is highly subjective in that there is very limited Scriptural evidence that these events actually occurred as described. Most of what Paul reports in this narrative are events inferred from passages found in his letters.

My purpose for this book is to help the reader gain a comprehensive overview of the activities related to development of the early Church, providing a satisfactory story line that flows from event to event.

My hope is that these narratives will provide some additional degree of reality to the events surrounding the expansion of the early Church, and thus make these happenings more understandable and acceptable as truth.

✛ ✛ ✛

I ask the reader to pardon any errors and/or weak assumptions, and thus enjoy my version of selected episodes related to the growth of the early Church.

The *Good News Bible* and *Good News for Modern Man* were used as the guiding source when quoting or paraphrasing.

✛ ✛ ✛

Discussion questions are found at the end of the book. These will hopefully encourage thoughtful inquiry regarding each narrative. Since I acknowledge that many, perhaps all of the narratives could be edited to represent a more reliable interpretation of the Scriptural events, I have added a last question to each narrative which states: *If you had written this narrative, how would the content of the story differ?*

Hopefully, readers' understandings will lead toward a more scripturally credible version of particular narratives. The author welcomes readers' feedback.

✛ ✛ ✛

Delbert Mueller
delmueller@att.net

Table of Contents

Narrator	Topic	Page
Mark	Events of Cyprus	1
Pomona	Antioch in Pisidia	11
Timothy	Iconium, Lystra, Derbe	15
James the Just	Jerusalem Council	23
Paul	Second journey with Silas	31
Luke	Gospel brought to Macedonia	37
Paul	Gospel brought to Achaia	45
Priscilla	Paul in Corinth	51
Apollos	Apollos in Ephesus	57
Demetrius	Riot in Ephesus	61
Silas	Review/Return to Jerusalem	69
Michael	Paul taken prisoner	73
Felix	Paul before Felix	85
Festus	Paul before Festus and Agrippa II	91
Luke	Paul to Rome	99
Paul	God's emissary to the Gentiles	109
Appendix A	Herod's Temple Mount	123
Appendix B	Map showing St. Paul's first missionary journey	124
Appendix C	Map showing St. Paul's second missionary journey	125
Appendix D	Map showing St. Paul's third missionary journey	126
Appendix E	Map showing St. Paul's travel to Rome	127

Then Mark Said

I am Mark, also known as John Mark, one of the many disciples of the Christ. At the time of our Lord's "earthly" ministry I was a *teenager*. I had been following Jesus for some time; following as a *junior disciple*. I'm the one who fled without his cloak when a soldier tried to stop me from escaping after Jesus had been captured in the Garden of Gethsemane.

My father's name was Jethro and my mother's name is Mary. Father died shortly after my *Day of Dedication*. Our family is wealthy. Father had a lucrative business arrangement with the Holy Temple. He was the sole purchaser of sacrificial animals for the Levites. His crew would scour the Judean countryside, looking for cattle, sheep, goats, pigeons, and doves that met Levitical law standards.

Farmers, shepherds, and columbary owners welcomed him; he offered a fair price. His philosophy was simple: Treat the seller fairly and he will enthusiastically receive you when you return. All of the animals purchased had to meet the strict standard required of sacrificial animals; they had to be, in every way, perfect specimens. These spiritual substitutes brought my father a fair but generous profit.

After a purchase, Father's workers would take the animals to one of the several corrals, pens, and cages he maintained near the Valley of Hinnom, just north of the infamous Potter's Field. Here the animals would be kept, waiting their selection as offerings to Yahweh. Birds were penned and as the need arose, carried through a designated corridor to the Court of Gentiles where they could be purchased as offerings.

Bulls, sheep, and goats were led through a specified entrance of the Temple, guided through the appropriate passageways, and prodded or carried up a series of inclines to a holding area just under the Court of Priests.

As required, Levites selected the designated animal, forced it through a second set of inclines leading to the slaughter floor, and began the bloody process of preparing sacrifice. That was the environment in which I grew up.

Some additional information: Barnabas, also called the Encourager, is my uncle; he and my mother are brother and sister. Our family has its roots in Cyprus. My grandparents were wealthy land owners. Upon their death the property was deeded to their first born son, my uncle. He, however, some weeks after that Pentecost Sunday, chose to sell it and give the money to the newly formed Christian Church in Jerusalem. My uncle was and still is a devoted missionary. His God-blessed efforts have led thousands to believe in Jesus as Lord and Savior. Allow me to tell you about some of them.

✠ ✠ ✠

The Church at Antioch (that is where the name Christian was first used to identify us) grew into a dynamic body of Christ's people. Many men stepped forward as prophets and teachers. Among them were my uncle Barnabas, Simeon (called the Black), Lucius (from Cyrene), Manaen (who had been brought up as a foster child with Herod Antipas), and Saul.

These leaders spent much of their independent time in prayer and frequent isolation from us; setting aside occasions for denial from food; a period of fasting. For me, one day became very special. I was permitted to join them. Much of this isolation-time was devoted to resolution of spiritual concerns. It was at such a moment as this that the question of sharing the good news of Jesus became a central topic. Manaen reminded, "Our Lord had commanded his disciples to 'go into all the world and preach the gospel to all people.'"

But such a challenge was not an easy undertaking. Simeon asked, "How do you prepare to go into a strange country with a message most have never heard? Where does one begin? How does one approach the locals? What would be the primary message? Lucius added, "I would be concerned about finding food and lodging. How could one be sure basic necessities would be provided?"

The group's solution: pray and fast . . . and let the Holy Spirit lead the action. I was allowed to stay. I know it sounds strange, but I could feel God's Spirit directing the Church to discover its duty. I could feel a conversion of thought and expression. As the conversation became more deliberative it pointed to my uncle and Saul as its respondents; finally, a decision.

Deacon Callis summarized, "We seem to be in agreement; commission Barnabas and Saul to begin our evangelical outreach on the Isle of Cyprus. It was believers from Cyprus and Cyrene who first brought the good news to us in Antioch almost ten years ago. We are indebted to them. We could, as was suggested, also have recommended Cyrene; however, it is too distant for a starting place. And there is another factor to consider: Barnabas has a connection with Cyprus. His family has roots there. People would remember Barnabas' parents and grandparents. He would not be an outsider, but rather accepted as returning family. And . . . since it was men from Cyprus who brought the Good News to us, we can assume there are Christian worshippers there. This is the ideal place to begin."

The issue was resolved. Barnabas and Saul would leave Antioch and become missionaries to Cyprus; and thanks be to God, I would go with them. I too would share the Good News with my Cypriot Jewish brothers and sisters.

✠ ✠ ✠

We left the port city of Seleucia midweek and arrived in Salamis the following afternoon. Our first job was to find lodging. This was easily accomplished. After limited inquiry we found a believer, Benjamin. Uncle expressed our relief, "We didn't expect to find believers in Cyprus so soon." Uncle asked about our family. Benjamin smiled, "You have a cousin who lives in Salamis. I will take you to him."

The home of Cousin Zebulon, his wife Hannah, and their three children became our home. We were blessed to have such gracious relatives; relatives who were also believers.

I asked our cousin, "How did you learn about Jesus? Who told you that he was the risen Messiah?" Zebulon responded, "We didn't always live in Seleucia. We used to live in Jerusalem. Hannah and I became believers on that Pentecost festival day; when so many were brought to faith and baptized. We were so happy – We had Jesus as our friend. Happy, that is until the persecution – You see, Hannah and I were present when our Deacon Stephen was stoned! It's hard to imagine . . . we both still have nightmares . . . and we will never forget it.

"For many of us, ninth-hour prayers in the Holy Temple were part of life. On that day as our prayers had ended and we were walking through a southern Huldah gate to descend the massive array of steps, we saw angry men dragging someone; it was Stephen! They pulled and pushed him past the south steps of the Temple and out of the city to an escarpment above the Kidron Valley. There they stoned him. It was terrible!"

Saul's response, "I know, I also was there."

✠ ✠ ✠

We shared our mission. Our time in Salamis was spent with Saul and Barnabas preaching in the neighboring synagogues each Sabbath, and as opportunity allowed, discussing the Good News of Jesus during the week. I was also introduced to preaching; a task I found a likable challenge. After a three week stay we felt a need to leave. There were other synagogues to visit; other souls to approach. We began to work our way across the island going from east to west along the Roman road, preaching and teaching as we went. Using the guidance provided by our newly found relatives and friends, each night we found fellow believers who provided us lodging.

After passing through Tremithorus we arrived in Kition. Imagine our surprise to discover Lazarus; yes, the Lazarus, the one our Lord had raised from death. He explained, "Following Jesus' resurrection I found it necessary to flee the Jerusalem area. My life was in danger. My sisters stayed in Bethany." We lodged with him for several weeks, helping the growing assembly of believers become an organized congregation. We left Kition with Lazarus as the recognized bishop of their church and headed for the cult-center of Amathus.

It was just a few more days until we reached Paphos. There we met the sorcerer Elymas – also named Bar-Jesus, a Jew who claimed to be a prophet. Elymas was an important person, serving as advisor to Lucius Sergius Paulus I, Rome's Proconsul of the island, and as president of a local synagogue.

Barnabas and Saul, as was their custom, attended each Sabbath worship. God's chance brought them to Elymas' synagogue. When Elymas learned that Saul was a highly educated Pharisee, he invited him to speak. Saul began his sermon with a review of Jewish history and concluded with a claim that a person named Jesus of Nazareth was the promised Messiah; risen from the dead . . . only believe and be baptized. The message *shook* the assembly. For a few – favorable reaction; for many – angry reaction – intense anger – fury – blasphemy!

Elymas was outraged – mostly embarrassed – humiliated – how could he have been so deceived – to invite blasphemy into the synagogue. "This man must pay! He must be taught a lesson!"

"Tie him to the pillar! Whip him! 39 lashes! Show him how we treat blasphemers!"

Paul preaching the Good News

Word spread like wildfire; such fierce behavior reached the ears of Proconsul Sergius Paulus. He called for Saul and Elymas to appear before him. Again, as he had done so many times before, Saul now instructed the Proconsul on our revolutionary Christian message. I could tell; the proconsul was impressed.

That reaction did not escape Elymas. He defended his action in the synagogue and condemned Saul and his message. "This Saul is trying to destroy the church of our Fathers! He teaches blasphemy! His teachings will turn friends into enemies; cause riots. He deserves your condemnation!"

That was too much for Saul. He turned on Elymas and said, "You son of the Devil! You are the enemy of everything that is good, and you always keep trying to turn the Lord's truths into lies! The Lord's hand will come down on you now; you will be blind and will not see the light of day for a time." At once Elymas cried out in fear, "My eyes! I can't see! All is dark! Help me! – Get me out of here! Take me home!"

The Proconsul was overwhelmed. His declaration: "Saul, no man has power to do what you just did! By your words you blinded Elymas! Your words have the power given only to gods! What you did could not be done except your god gave you the authority. No Roman god could do that! You have convinced me – I believe! Your words and that miracle have made me a believer. What you say must be true! Your Jesus of Nazareth is a risen Messiah; a god with power.

"You have changed me; and I Paulus will change you. You shall no longer be called by your Hebrew name, Saul. From now on all men shall call you by your Roman name. Just as I am called Paulus, so your name shall be Paul."

We stayed as guests of the Proconsul for several days; using this time to help him understand the Christ. But we needed to leave. The pressing question for us now was, "Where do we go next?" All was settled when Sergius Paulus talked about his family in Pisidian Antioch. "As you know, we Proconsuls are shifted from one locale to another on call of Rome. I started in Pisidia, but now am on Cyprus. I have many relatives in Pisidia. I would be forever indebted to you men if you were to go to Pisidian Antioch and share the good news of Jesus. If you choose to go there, I will provide a letter of introduction."

We sailed for the seaport city of Perga, Pamphilyia. Upon arrival Paul immediately began preparations to move up into the country-side. This meant we would soon leave Perga and trek into the treacherous Taurus Mountains. I began to hear stories; stories of what lay ahead; scary stories. People started to warn us; warn us of the dangers: the climb; the cold; but most of all, the bandits. Not only did these godless steal, they killed or ransomed. I feared, "That could happen to me."

Among those who warned us, were two men in armor. "Your best bet is to cross over following the Sebaste Way, but it's dangerous; we made it, but not without a fight. The gods were with us. We were about a day's journey from here when it happened. As we turned past an outcrop and into a narrow ravine, there they stood . . . four blood-thirsty, gnarly bandits; sword in one hand, knife in the other, ready to attack. Their big mistake – neglecting to reconnoiter – they anticipated travelers like you three. But we are soldiers. We were mounted on war horses. They were no match for us. We unsheathed our swords and charged. The ravine was narrow. There was no place to run. We each sliced one bandit; the horses did the rest with their hoofs. We turned, dismounted, bridled our mounts, and assured the bandits were dead; then pulled the bodies to the side, and left. Had we not been soldiers on war horses, we would probably have had all our valuables taken, and possibly been beheaded. That is the way of the bandit here."

Early the next day I approached Paul. "I cannot go with you and Barnabas. It's too dangerous; I'm afraid; I'm not brave like you are."

I don't like to talk about what followed. Let it suffice that Barnabas understood and Paul was disappointed; and I think angry. They would proceed without me. I boarded the next available ship and returned to Antioch. – It was hard to forgive myself.

Mark: Mark 14:51-52; Luke 12:12
Cyprus ministry: Acts 13:1-13

Then Pomona Said

I am Pomona, wife of Lucius Sergius Paulus II, and daughter-in-law to Lucius Sergius Paulus I, who is Proconsul over Cyprus. We live in Pisidian Antioch, about a four to five day trek from the seaport, Perga. Our two cities are connected by the Roman Sebaste Way. My husband and I are large land owners. Some would call us moneyed. Until recently, we would have said, "We dutifully worship our gods and they reward our veneration and loyalty." But all that changed. We changed . . . soon after Paul and Barnabas arrived. The letter of introduction from my father-in-law was sufficient for us to invite them to share our home. And they also shared . . . shared more; so much more. They arrived on a Thursday. Friday was spent showing them around the town and getting to know them and their backgrounds. I was fascinated as they talked about their lives. We soon discovered that they were on a mission, and we were part of that mission; details would follow.

✠ ✠ ✠

An early concern directed us to the local synagogue. We introduced the three to the rabbi. He was excited to learn that men had come all the way from Jerusalem and Antioch to his synagogue. Paul assured the rabbi that they would attend worship the following day. As it turned out, so did we.

This was a new experience for us. Lucius and I had not attended synagogue worship before. It was a fascinating experience. It began with the *Shema*, "Hear O Israel, the Lord is our God, the Lord is One;" words from their Torah. It continued with prayer to the God of Abraham, Isaac, and Jacob. Next came a reading from the prophets. The worship highlight was a sermon. As expected, since Paul was a visiting Pharisee, he was asked to speak. His message was exceedingly challenging to all present. The first part covered four main points: God is the God of the people of Israel; God chose the patriarchs for Himself; God redeemed His people from Egypt, leading them through the desert; God gave them the land of Palestine as an inheritance.

Paul then began to shift his focus to a Jew named Jesus of Nazareth, a descendent of King David. He called on both Israelites and those proselytized Gentiles present to accept this Jesus as the prophet's promised Messiah. He would be God's instrument of redemption for all people; freedom from the plague of sin. Paul asserted that while Jesus was on earth he was rejected by the Jerusalem church leaders. They regarded him as a blasphemer and caused him to be crucified on a cross. Paul preached, "This Messiah submitted to death on a cross; becoming the sacrifice for all the sins from which the Law of Moses could not set you free. I invite everyone present to become a believer; to accept Jesus as your risen Messiah."

When Paul finished speaking, Barnabas whispered to me, "This is the very same message Paul shared with your father-in-law." It was very convincing.

As we left the synagogue we were followed by a crowd; they wanted more. During the following week, various gathering places, including our house, were filled with Jews and proselytized Gentiles looking for additional spiritual direction.

The next Sabbath was a bit *crazy*. The synagogue was filled to overflowing; *standing room only*. That did not *set well* with the Jewish leadership. Fear was expressed, "See how this Paul draws such a great crowd?" Another conveyed his frustration, "What is so appealing about him?" A third answered, "It's simply this: It's not the man that draws the crowd, it's his message. He claims adherence to the Law of Moses should no longer be the focus of our faith; but rather a belief in that Jesus person." A fourth responded, "If that is the case, anybody will be welcome, and that will allow the unspeakable: Even uncircumcised Gentiles will be permitted to worship with us. Soon the entire city will be converted to this Paul's version of Judaism. That must not happen!"

Among those most infuriated, certain Gentile women of high social standing. They considered themselves of high reputation in part because they had married favorably; having wealthy Jewish men or proselytized Gentiles as husbands. Being married to circumcised men had value. They led a campaign of persecution to force Paul and Barnabas out of our city. My husband and I were not part of this retched action.

As we and fellow believers walked with Paul and Barnabas out of the city, Barnabas said to us, "Lucius and Pomona, we thank our God for you; you have remained our friends throughout this challenging, yet victorious visit. – And to all who walk with us we say, "As we shake the dust of the city off our feet in protest, know this, my fellow believers; you are exempt from this act. To you we send God's Holy Spirit. May the Spirit strengthen you and bring you joy."

They left with our blessing. We pray they will return.

✠ ✠ ✠

Pisidian Antioch: Acts 13:14-52

Then Timothy Said

I am Timothy, a young man and citizen of Lystra in Lycaonia. Even though my mother Eunice and grandmother Lois are Jews, I was not circumcised; my Gentile father forbade it. He insisted that I remain a true Greek. While Father was unrelenting on that major point of identity, he did support my mother's efforts to teach me the Torah and the writings of the prophets. The result of his benevolence: even as a child I tried to follow the Laws of Moses and honor the Sabbath and the major festivals. Father even joined with us in our family's celebration of the Passover. He was a caring parent who supported and provided well. I grew up in comfort. – Our great house, surrounding a large inner patio, provided my every need.

We, that is my mother, grandmother, and I first met Paul and Barnabas in the synagogue. Paul was the honored guest; the Sabbath day speaker. They had recently, after an extended preaching tour, arrived from Iconium in Phrygia and its surrounding regions. They both showed signs of wear; each claimed sufferings from stoning.

Paul and Barnabas spoke forcefully about a person called Jesus of Nazareth. The message attracted wide attention. Their primary teaching was that Jesus of Nazareth was the promised

Messiah who though innocent, was hung on a cross outside Jerusalem and died. The miracle to their story was that three days later, he rose from death, showed himself to hundreds of people, and finally ascended into the heavens. They taught that this Messiah suffered death on a cross to pay the penalty for all of the world's sin, both Jew and Greek. They declared that this freedom from the punishment of sin applied to all who believed the story they told. All one had to do for eternal salvation was accept that Jesus is the risen Messiah; nothing more. – The demands of the Torah no longer applied. – Several Jews and Gentiles became believers.

Paul and Barnabas spent much of each day inviting discussions that led to *Messiah talk*. One day, as Paul was sharing the Messiah message, he stood near a man who was lame from birth. The lame man sat listening intensely to the words being spoken . . . and he believed. I watched the event. I could see Paul take particular notice of the man. He stopped his sermon, looked hard at the man and said, "Sir, stand up straight on your feet!" Immediately the lame man's face brightened and he sprang to his feet – and stood. He began to walk and jump . . . run and skip . . . laugh and yell . . . shout with joy! It was mind boggling – one minute a cripple . . . next minute totally ambulatory – a miracle! A real miracle!

Most of us Lystra residents are bilingual; speaking Greek and Lycaonium. A crowd began to gather. They saw the man. He had been a cripple – but not now . . . now they saw him run and jump – they heard him shout . . . and they joined in. Using their Lycoanian language they announced, "The gods have visited us! The gods have become like men and have come down to us! Zeus and Hermes have appeared to us." A crowd gathered . . . excitement all around! People yelling and singing and praying!

A parade began to form. Paul and Barnabas became its

reluctant participants. The horde advanced toward the city gate. A temple dedicated to Zues was located outside the town. As the throng edged toward it they were joined by several temple priests and their assistants towing sacrificial bulls. Following them were priestesses carrying bouquets of flowers and declaring, "The gods have come to honor our temple. Praise be to Zues! Glory be to Hermes! Worship our gods! Adore our gods!"

The chief priest approached Paul. The crowd hesitated. He bowed . . . reverently and spoke. "Great god Hermes, we reverence and worship you as priest to Zues. We ask that you speak a message of hope for us."

He then turned to Barnabas, knelt in obeisance with his forehead touching the ground. He raised his head and spoke again, "Great and mighty Zues, there is no other god as notable and mighty as you. We ask that you sanctify our temple by entering into its sanctuary and consecrating it with your presence. It is to you, O Zues, and your spokes-person Hermes that we wish to offer the sacrifices we have brought."

I continued to watch. Paul and Barnabas were visibly distressed. – Outraged! What would they do? – They tore their clothes and ran into the crowd, shouting, "Why are you doing this? We ourselves are only human beings like you! We are not gods! We are messengers here to announce the Good News, to turn you away from these worthless things you honor, to the living God who made heaven, earth, sea, and all that is in them. You must change; do away with your man-created religion; your man-made gods of stone and metal.

"We proclaim the living God. In the past this God allowed all people to go their own way. But he has not ignored you. He has always given evidence of his existence by the good things he does; he gives you rain from heaven and crops at the right times; he gives you food and fills your hearts with happiness. This is the God we proclaim."

Even with these words Paul and Barnabas could hardly keep the crowd from offering a sacrifice to them.

The temple chief priest was not pleased. He was deeply embarrassed – He asked his assistants, "Have I been duped? If these men are not gods, who are they? Are they imposters? No, they performed a miracle. The people saw it. Are they priests of a foreign god? – We were about to sacrifice to them. They spoke inflammatory words against our gods. Does their presence defile our temple? What should I do?"

I did not wait to see what would happen next. I ran to Paul and Barnabas and urged them to follow me; they needed to disappear before the crowd could coalesce into a violent mob and act. We fled through side streets until we reached my parent's home. No one followed; they could hide out here; they would be safe.

The next Sabbath found our family, including Father, attending the synagogue. Paul and Barnabas were with us. After the readings, Paul was again asked to speak. His theme continued to be: "Jesus of Nazareth is the risen Messiah." As he was speaking, I watched. There were new faces in the synagogue. Outsiders; men I had not seen before; men who by their expressions I could interpret as enemies of Paul.

Their agitations grew as Paul declared, "Salvation is through faith in the sacrifice of Jesus." When Paul declared, "For Gentiles, the laws of the Torah are no longer necessary for salvation; faith alone saves," their anger broke into action. They ran forward and pushed Paul aside. First began the accusations; then the mêlée. They shouted, "This Paul speaks against the Laws of Moses. He will tell you that there is no need to circumcise; to obey the Sabbath laws; to have sacrifices offered daily in our holy Jerusalem Temple. Allow him to continue this preaching and all we hold in high honor, all the traditions of our fathers he will tramp under his feet. He is a blasphemer! He deserves death! Death by stoning!"

Before we realized what was happening, the men grabbed Paul and dragged him through the door of the synagogue and outside the town gate. He was thrown to the ground and lay there. Stones began to fly; Paul was hit in the chest; then on the lower abdomen; next on the leg; then in the head. He dropped to the ground, unconscious.

More rocks were about to be thrown when Father intervened. "What are you men doing? Do you realize that the man you are stoning is a Roman citizen? Do you have any idea what will happen to you if the civil authorities learn of this action? *Where are your brains?* – Perhaps you are lucky! Perhaps he is not dead, but merely unconscious! If he is not dead, this act need not be reported. If he is dead, the justice of Roman law will destroy you! – I see him move. – Get out from here! Leave! Run! Now!

Paul woke, and after a long delay to clear his head, struggled to be upright and returned with us to our house; aches and all. My mother salved the wounds as best she could. Paul spent the Sabbath resting. The next day he and Barnabas left Lystra for Derbe with our blessing.

It was almost a month before we saw Paul and Barnabas again. They had begun to backtrack; visiting towns previously visited. They reported a successful stay in Derbe; resulting in many conversions to Christianity. We reported our progress, "This past month has not been easy. We have been ostracized and demonized by those Jews and proselytes who consider us an evil cult. But God has greatly blessed us. Our congregation has grown to over one hundred believers. We meet each Sabbath in our house; the patio is large.

"However, we need advice; organization is missing. We have no agreed-to leadership. We want you to help us identify men who will be our spiritual guides. Help us become organized as did the Jerusalem church and your home church in Antioch."

Paul's reply, "Before we left Derbe, we helped the congregation appoint leaders. We will help you do the same. This is the list of qualifications we established. You will need to identify men who are regarded as of high character, have only one wife, are self-controlled and orderly, willing to welcome strangers, are able to teach, are not drunkards or violent, but gentle and peaceful, and must not love money."

The members prayed and fasted. God guided our choice; seven elders were selected and commended to the Lord.

Paul and Barnabas left, intending to pass through the territory of Pisidia again and on to Perga. From there they planned to reach Attalia and sail back to their home church in Antioch. Their first missionary tour would be complete.

Antioch in Pisidia, Lystra, Derbe/Return
to Antioch in Syria: Acts 14:1-28
Standards for church leaders: 1Timothy 3:2-4

Then James the Just Said

I am James, the half brother of Jesus of Nazareth and second son of Joseph and Mary. They call me the Just One. I was educated to become a rabbi. After attending the Yeshiva, our local area school, and shortly after my *Day of Dedication*, I was selected to attend the Abraham Joshua Rabbinical Boarding School in Tiberius. A scholarship allowed me to continue studies at the School of Hillel in Jerusalem where the esteemed Rabbi Gamaliel was my proctor. I had reason to believe that soon I would be deemed worthy of membership in an area Sanhedrin. Such an election would fulfill my life's dream.

I was an unbeliever – that is, until his resurrection. Following that earth-shaking event I was among his strongest supporters. I suppose it was because of my family's relationship with Jesus, and because I was a rabbi, that I was chosen to be the leader of the Jerusalem Church. Such was my role when Paul and Barnabas arrived in Jerusalem with a problem; a very serious problem.

Soon after Paul and Barnabas, along with other men from the Antioch church, arrived in Jerusalem, I called a meeting of the Council. The various parties were introduced; Peter and John were present. Upon completion of these formalities, I called the Council to order and presented the single issue before us: Must Gentile Christians submit to the Torah? Both sides would be heard. I first asked Paul and Barnabas to offer background. Barnabas became the spokesperson.

"Paul and I were sent by the church at Antioch in Syria to evangelize men and women in Cyprus. Our journey did not end there; it reached all the way into Pisidia and Lycaonia. Our work was greatly blessed; many Jews and Gentiles were converted to Christ. The Antioch congregation that sent us is made up of both Jews and Gentiles; that biethnic relationship has created an unresolved tension. You see, not all Christian Gentiles have submitted to the Torah. The tension facing us in Antioch is this: What does God require of Gentile believers?

"When our *mixed* congregation commissioned Paul and me to be missionaries, it was implied that we would proclaim the Good News to both ethnic groups; with the understanding that some who converted would become Gentiles Christians and others would be Jewish Christians.

"Upon our return, the stress that had been troubling the Antioch congregation now became our controversy. The dividing question was: Should Gentile Christians be required to obey the Torah? Should they be forced to become *Jewish-Gentile Christians*? Paul and I did not believe such a requirement necessary, and ministered from that position."

Barnabas continued, "This single issue initiated a major dispute when men from the Jerusalem church came to Antioch and insisted, 'You cannot be saved unless you are circumcised as the Law of Moses requires.' Paul and I got into a fierce argument with these men about this. The disagreement became a congregation-wide dispute; early resolution was critically necessary. The Antioch church council met. They ruled that the matter involved universal church policy and could not be treated as local disagreement. It must rather be decided in Jerusalem by the apostles and elders of the *Mother* Church. The congregation agreed to send Paul and me, along with some of our Antioch brothers, to Jerusalem. The question will have to be resolved here; by you men."

My response, "Before we proceed further, I want to give Paul and Barnabas an opportunity to share the history of their work so that we may better understand the cause from which this concern rises." Paul and Barnabas told of the church in Cyprus and the new converts, both Jew and Gentile. They shared their success story with Sergius Paulus, the governor. They then told of their decisions to travel to Pamphylia, Pisidia, and Lycaonia, and the dangers and successes they experienced, especially the successes among the Gentiles.

When they began to talk about baptizing uncircumcised Gentiles, their report was interrupted. Several Pharisee believers demanded, "You do not have permission to do this! Gentiles must be circumcised and told to obey the Law of Moses! We cannot allow uncircumcised Gentiles to worship with law abiding Jews. There must be one rule for all. Christ is the Jewish Messiah; he died for the sins of his Jewish people; not for the uncircumcised. Gentile believers who wish to be saved must submit to the Law of Moses as do all believing Jews. Only then will they be rescued; only then can they be accepted into the church."

The debate became more heated. Some insisting that submission to the Law and believing in a risen Savior was the route to paradise. Others contending that when Christ died on the cross he became the fulfillment of the Law; the final sacrifice; the Law no longer bound them.

At this point Peter got up and offered his firm opinion. "My brothers, you know that a long time ago God chose me from among you to preach the Good News to the Gentiles, so that they could hear and believe. And God who knows the thoughts of everyone showed his approval of the Gentiles by giving the Holy Spirit to them, just as he had to us. He made no difference between us and them; he forgave their sins because they believed. So then, why do you now want to put God to the test by laying a load on the backs of the believers which neither our ancestors nor we ourselves were able to carry? No! We believe and are saved by the grace of the Lord Jesus, just as they are."

The room was silent. You could *hear a pin drop*. The quiet was broken by Barnabas and Paul. They used this calm as an opportunity to report all the miracles and wonders that God had performed through them among the Gentiles. That was enough. No counter argument was heard. The room was again silent. I used this as a signal to speak.

I rose and faced the Council. "Listen to me, my brothers! Simon has just explained how God first showed his care for the Gentiles by taking from among them a people to belong to him. The words of the prophets agree completely with this. Scripture says:

> *After this I will return, says the Lord, and restore the kingdom of David. I will rebuild its ruins and make it strong again. And so all the rest of mankind will come to me, all the Gentiles whom I have called to be my own. So says the Lord, who made this known long ago.*

"It is my opinion," I continued, "that we should not trouble the Gentiles who are turning to God. After listening to all arguments – pro and con – I suggest the following: Instead of forcing the same restrictions of the Torah upon the Gentiles that we Jews accept, we should write a letter that imposes only the following few restrictions. They are:

> *not to eat any food that is ritually unclean because*
> *it has been offered to idols;*
> *to keep themselves from sexual immorality;*
> *not to eat any animal that has been strangled;*
> *not to eat any blood.*

These four limitations are necessary. If Gentile believers are to break bread and partake in the Lord's Supper with Jewish believers, food must not become a divisive ingredient. But we also cannot advise our Jewish Christians to abandon their traditions, for the Laws of Moses has been read for a very long time in the synagogues every Sabbath and its words are preached in every town. We must honor that tradition. And all will agree that sexual immorality as practiced by many unbelieving Gentiles cannot be practiced amongst us." With that, the matter was settled.

After further discussion, final agreement was reached. A letter would be written and delivered to the Church in Antioch. Paul and Barnabas would return to Antioch accompanied by Judas called Barsabbas and Silas, both highly respected men, carrying a letter from the Jerusalem Church to all Gentiles. The letter read:

> *We, the apostles and the elders, your brothers,*
> *send greetings to all our brothers of Gentile birth*
> *who live in Antioch, Syria, and Cilicia. We have*
> *heard that some men who went from our groups*
> *have troubled and upset you by what they said;*
> *they had not, however, received any instruction*
> *from us. And so we have met together and have*
> *all agreed to choose some messengers and send*
> *them to you. They will go with our dear friends*

Barnabas and Paul, who have risked their lives in the service of our Lord Jesus Christ. We send you, then, Judas and Silas, who will tell you in person the same things we are writing. The Holy Spirit and we have agreed not to put any other burden on you besides these necessary rules: eat no food that has been offered to idols; eat no blood; eat no animal that has been strangled; and keep yourselves from sexual immorality. You will do well if you take care not to do these things. With our best wishes.

The letter was received with joy and encouragement in Antioch; copies were prepared and carried to neighboring churches. Barnabas and Paul remained in Antioch for some time.

✛ ✛ ✛

The Jerusalem Council meets: Acts 15:1-35
James' quotation: Amos 9:11-12
Laws of Moses: Exodus 34:15-17; Leviticus 18:6-23; 17:10-16

Then Paul Said

I am Paul, a Jew and a Roman citizen from Tarsus in Cilicia, a city of some repute.

Most of the citizens of Tarsus are committed to serving the god Mithras, a religion whose roots can be traced to the Persian faith of Zoroastrianism. I am a Pharisee. I worship Yahweh. I trace my ancestry to King Saul and the tribe of Benjamin. I take pride in being a Pharisee and the son of a Pharisee. I studied at the feet of Rabban Gamaliel, once president of the Jerusalem Sanhedrin. When necessary, I earn a living as a tent maker.

I was an ardent protector of the Jewish faith; earned a reputation as an unrelenting persecutor of those who opposed it; those who regarded Jesus of Nazareth as Messiah. I was ahead of most fellow Jews of my age in my practice of the Jewish religion, and was much more devoted to the tradition of our ancestors.

All of this changed about sixteen years previous to today, following a life altering experience as I and my companions traveled from Jerusalem to Damascus. I had a vision; a light shown down from heaven! A voice spoke to me chiding:

Saul, Saul, why do you persecute me?

It was Jesus talking to me and telling me to stop opposing him;

telling me to be a spokesperson for him. – I had to obey. – I became a new person. I had been wrong . . . terribly wrong. In that moment I was transferred from being an enemy of Jesus of Nazareth to becoming a disciple of Jesus; one who now regarded him as the risen Messiah; as the Lord and Savior of the world!

Former friends and co-workers could not understand what happened. No explanation proved satisfactory. Not only did I now personally confess Jesus as the risen Messiah, I began to teach that truth to others. I contradicted my former teachings. I was perceived as a traitor; a turncoat . . . a blasphemer . . . one worthy of death by stoning.

I would have been killed, except for my new friends, Ananias and the other Damascus believers. They helped me escape the city. For the next three years, I wandered about Arabia searching my heart to better understand the meaning of my conversion; I asked: "What was God's plan as proclaimed in the life, death, resurrection, and ascension of his Son? What was to be my life's purpose in this plan?"

God guided me to an understanding that reached beyond anything I could have prayed for and have expected. But God's revelation to me did not end there. During the years since I left Jerusalem, returned to Tarsus, and was brought to Antioch in Syria by Barnabas, God revealed to me a secret held from the prophets of old; namely this: That by means of the Gospel, the Gentiles have a part with the Jews in God's blessings. They are members of the same body and share in the promise that God made through Christ Jesus. And my calling was to be a messenger of this new Gospel.

My first journey had ended some time ago. I was eager to begin another journey; one that would lead through Cilicia and

Pisidia, and Phrygia. I was anxious to again share the Good News with those I had earlier helped come to faith. Barnabas, while having a desire to return to Cyprus, agreed to join me on this other route; but he wanted to have his nephew John Mark join us.

That I could not agree to. My point, "John Mark is too immature for this journey. It will take us through mountains more dangerous than our travel north from Perga. Mark's focus is on sharing the Good News with Jews; he is not ready for the vulnerabilities we will experience following actions such as baptizing uncircumcised Gentiles. I do not believe he is ready for this kind of challenge."

Words were exchanged between Barnabas and me. Some rather unkind words, I fear. Yet, our disagreement was on what is a best course of action, not on personal condemnation. And we both had Mark's best interests at heart.

Finally, Barnabas said, "My friend, let us agree on a plan that will allow us to remain friends. I will take Mark with me to Cyprus; a region we both believe is relatively safe. Mark is a good man, and this second venture will help him grow and mature in mission. You choose another who is willing to undertake the rigor of your plan; I suggest Silas."

With that we parted friends; each carrying the message of salvation to different quarters of the Roman world. For Barnabas and me – regretfully, our paths would never cross again; for Mark and me – together in Rome.

✠ ✠ ✠

Since our return from Jerusalem, Silas had become a close and dear friend; a man of high character and fervent in ministry to the saints. Though a Jew, such as I, he held a passionate desire to bring as many Gentiles to faith as the Lord had chosen.

Silas and I sailed for Tarsus with commendation by the believers. After a brief stop with relatives and friends, we visited each of the churches in Syria and Cilicia that I had helped begin. At each church we shared the ruling of the Jerusalem Council. From there we continued up through the Cilician Gates of the Taurus Mountains. The route was difficult but beautiful. Before proceeding to Derbe, we chose to visit a region known as Cappadocia. It included a community that lived in caves cut out of a soft tuff mountain rock. This former center of Hittite power housed a synagogue. When we left after a two week stay, we thanked God for establishing a Christian congregation among these mountain carved homes.

Our visit to Derbe was gratifying. The church had grown; the leadership was stable; souls were being saved. After sharing the ruling of the Jerusalem Council we left for Lystra. How pleasant to be with these special believers. We had experienced such trials here. But time heals; the uproar about Zues and Hermes was all but forgotten. Many former Zues worshipers had joined the Christian congregation. The Jerusalem Council ruling was again shared.

We lodged with young Timothy's father, his mother Eunice, and Grandmother Lois. Eunice was a Jew, but Timothy's father Andrew was Greek. As we shared stories about our travels, an anxious Timothy interrupted. "I want to go with you! I want to become a missionary for Jesus Christ." An intense family debate ensued. I was asked my opinion. "I would welcome Timothy. He is a strong, steady young Christian man. He would be an asset to us. But there is one thing I need to insist upon. Timothy will have to be circumcised." Such a requirement startled the family. "Why? You told us that Gentiles are not required to submit to circumcision; Timothy is one-half Gentile. Shouldn't he be exempt?"

My response was reasoned, "Ordinarily I would agree. But

since he is going to be working with both Jews and Gentiles, and since the community knows that you, Andrew, are Greek, we must do our best to not offend the Jewish communities of this region. And when we leave here and preach in other towns, I fear that if Timothy is not circumcised, his teachings will be rejected by the Jews he is trying to convert. There are Jews, who upon learning that Timothy is allowed to remain uncircumcised, would do all in their power to defame his ministry. That situation we want to avoid."

The debate continued until Andrew announced, "Timothy is of age. He can make decisions for himself. If he agrees, he has my permission to be circumcised. And he has my permission to join Paul and Silas."

The matter was settled. After a one week stay, Silas and I, with Timothy, left for Iconium and Antioch.

Beginning of the second journey: Acts 15:36-16:5
God's secret: Ephesians 3:6-7

Then Luke Said

I am Luke, born a Roman citizen of Greek parents in Antioch, Syria. I am by profession a physician, educated at that famous Medical School of Tarsus, Darius Atossa. It was in Tarsus that I met Paul. We became close friends, and as our friendship grew, brothers in Christ. I was one of those who carried the Good News of Jesus Christ to my home town. Our message became one of several seeds that blossomed into a vibrant Christian church. Paul served as one of our leaders; brought to us by Barnabas. Professional responsibilities separated us for a time. I traveled a good deal as a ship's doctor. However, we met again in Troas, were separated after Philippi, and finally together once more in Troas when Paul returned to Macedonia on his third journey. It was here that I helped Paul write his second letter to the church in Corinth. We remained together until Paul's death.

So many ministries happened after Troas. Listen as I tell you about some of them.

✛ ✛ ✛

This first event took place in Philippi, a city of the first district of Macedonia and a Roman colony. I was at this time no longer a sailor's doctor, but rather practicing my profession in Troas. Paul and his entourage had left Antioch in Pisidia and reached

Mysia. They planned to go into Bithynia, but the Spirit of Jesus intervened. They learned from casual conversation that I was living in Troas. That information was enough to convince Paul to change his plans and journey to greet me.

What a joy to be with him again! He and his friends lodged with me. We talked and shared. I confessed, "I enjoy my work here, Paul, but don't plan to make Troas my permanent home. In fact, I find myself wanting to do as you are doing; become an evangelist for Christ. There are so many souls to reach. I know of no one in Macedonia or Achaia who follows *The Way*. Most of Rome is ignorant of the Good News. You can't do it all by yourself; you will need helpers."

That comment sparked Paul's imagination. "All right then. Why don't you join us? We can always use another person. And given the number of the sores and bruises I have received over the past years, a good doctor may be just what I need. – Let's pray about this." – We did.

The next morning as we came together for breakfast, Paul burst into the room and announced. "We are going to Macedonia! Last night I had a vision. I saw a man, a Macedonian standing before me and begging, 'Come over to Macedonia and help us.' We must go. The Lord wills it!" The matter was settled; and I would go with them.

Our ship sailed straight across from Troas to Samothrace, and the next day to Neapolis. From there we went inland to the Macedonian city of Philippi, also a Roman colony. We found accommodations near the home of a faithful Jewish widow named Lydia. She and her late husband had moved to Philippi from the town of Thyatira. They had established a profitable business as dealers in purple dyed cloth, a trade which had flourished in their native province from ancient days. Lydia now ran the business. Since she was a Jew, and the city was mostly Greek, we found comfort through our visits with her. She told us that there was no synagogue in Philippi, but prayer services were held each Sabbath at a site bordering the river that ran through the town. We were invited to join Lydia and her friends at the prayer site.

The prayer service was led by an elderly Jewish man, a close friend of Lydia. When he learned that Paul, a Pharisee, had joined the group, he immediately requested that Paul share a message. His sermon's central teaching was simple: Jesus of Nazareth is the promised Messiah. His suffering and death paid the penalty for all sin for all people. Those who trust this truth are forgiven of all their sins and destined for heaven. Paul's message was spoken with a power; with compelling persuasion.

Lydia believed and became the first Macedonian Christian. Shortly after, her family also confessed their acceptance. There was great joy in the house – and a fervent request. "We want to be baptized." It was done. – After all who confessed belief were baptized, Lydia offered this invitation, "Come and stay in my house if you have decided that I am a true believer in the Lord." We did.

What followed next was not expected. We continued our stay in Philippi; Paul and Silas using each day to declare Jesus Christ the promised Messiah. One Sabbath day as we were going to the place of prayer we were met by a slave girl, half-dressed, mired in dirt with a head of straggled hair. Friends warned us, "Watch out for her. This wench has an evil spirit. It enables her to tell the future. This generously bosomed *fortune teller* has earned a lot of money for her owners." --She suddenly ran toward us. As she approached she shouted, "These men are servants of the Most High God! They announce to you how you can be saved!" We ignored her and she was guided away by her owners.

On each of the following days, as we talked to people about *The Way*, she would find us and follow us, repetitively yelling words similar to those yelled before: "These Jewish men serve the Most High God! They are telling you how to be saved!" Since Timothy and I were identified as Gentiles, we were exempt from the woman's frenzy. The ranting continued day-after-day, increasing in fervor each time she encountered us. Her interrupting behavior became a major hindrance. The constant ravings began to suggest that her insanity was somehow connected with Paul and Silas' message. Citizens turned away, associating our Gospel message with her lunatic behaviors. Finally, the day came when Paul had enough. As she was repeatedly shouting her mantra about "these Jewish men," Paul stopped all conversation, turned and stood in silence. He then looked the woman *straight-in-the-eye* and loudly demanded the evil spirit within her, "In the name of Jesus Christ I order you to come out of her!" – At that very moment she was sane.

But that was not the end of it. Her owners were enraged; Paul had destroyed their source of income. Within minutes there was an assault on my friends. Paul and Silas were dragged into the public square. Local Roman authorities were summoned. Accusations were pronounced, "These men are Jews, and they are causing trouble in our city. They are teaching customs that are against our law. We are Roman citizens, and can neither accept these customs nor practice them." A mob scene erupted. Calls such as, "Traitors! Blasphemers! Jews! False Teachers! Away with them!" were heard. There was no trial – gang mentality took over. The officials tore the clothes off Paul and Silas and ordered them to be whipped. After several beatings, they were thrown into the local jail with the order,

"Lock them up tight." We heard the jailer brag, "I threw them into the inner cell and fastened their feet between heavy blocks of wood. They're not going anywhere." Timothy and I stayed near.

Timothy stood vigil while I informed Lydia of the trouble. She sent food back with me. We ate; darkness covered us; we waited outside the jail. We could hear singing coming from inside the jail. The voices belonged to Paul and Silas. I thought, "What great men of faith they are." It had been a hard day and we were exhausted. We slept. – I awoke; the earth was shaking. I cried, "Earthquake!" I yelled to Timothy, "Go to the middle of the street! Get away from walls! They may fall!" I saw the jailer run toward the jail gate. He surveyed the scene; saw rubble where the jail gate should be, and moaned, "They have escaped! My prisoners have escaped!" I saw him draw his sword. He was going to do that honorable final act; suicide. – Then a sharp call, "Put down your sword! Don't kill yourself! We are still in the prison! We have not escaped!" It was Paul's voice coming from inside the jail. A light was called for. Paul and Silas climbed up and over the twisted prison gate; each showed several bruises. The jailer came trembling, fell to his knees and confessed, "Forgive me! I am Nathan the chief jailer. The earthquake was a miracle! A real miracle! – Often during these past weeks I heard you speak about your Messiah. I didn't believe you. . . . But all that has changed. Now I do. . . . This earthquake happened for a reason. Your God is calling me. He wants me to be a believer. . . .

And I want to. – Sirs, what must I do to be saved?" The answer was immediate, "Believe on the Lord Jesus, and you will be saved – you and your family."

The streets were beginning to fill with people. There was mass confusion. Several houses had collapsed. Thankfully, no one was killed; but several were hurt by falling rubble. Our jailer friend quickly ordered that the other prisoners be herded into a portion of the jail that was least damaged and held until morning light. He then guided us into his house. It was not damaged. Everyone was up and awake; no one was hurt.

The jailer's wife washed the wounds the men had suffered and gave them food. Time was taken to expand on the salvation message. I could tell that the saving message was believed. All present were filled with joy as they confessed their belief in Jesus Christ as Lord and Savior. . . . And all were baptized. A short early morning's sleep followed.

Later that morning there was a visit from the local police with the order, "Let those men go." The message was passed to Paul. "The officials have sent an order for you and Silas to be released. You may leave, then, and go in peace." Paul's response, "Go in peace? We were not found guilty of any crime, yet we were whipped in public – and we are Roman citizens! Then we were thrown in prison. And now they want to send us away secretly? *No way*! The Roman officials themselves must come here and formally let us out."

These words were reported to the Roman officials; and when they heard that Paul and Silas were Roman citizens, they were afraid. Soon men arrived. "Brothers, we apologize for yesterday and last night. We did not know you were citizens. We thought you ordinary Jews. Our deepest regrets; we cannot undo the wretched treatment you received from us. We can only ask your forgiveness and that you not press charges. We offer you our blessing and ask that you peacefully leave our city."

Paul's retort, "First, you will join us as we visit with Lydia. She must understand the details of what happened here and be assured of no repeat persecution on your part."

Our visit helped encourage the believers at Lydia's house; they felt safe to practice their faith. The Roman officials offered that assurance.

Paul, Silas, and Timothy departed for Thessalonica. I remained behind.

✠ ✠ ✠

From Troas to Philippi: Acts 16:6-40

Then Paul Said

I am Paul, a Jew, a Pharisee, a Roman citizen, and a herald for Jesus Christ the Messiah. You met me before.

✠ ✠ ✠

My stay in Thessalonica was short; lasted just three Sabbaths. The city had a synagogue. I became the featured Sabbath speaker and my message the center of attention. I preached, "Jesus is the promised Messiah. The Scriptures teach that he had to suffer and rise from death. The Messiah is not an earthly ruler, but rather a suffering servant; our substitute. He paid the penalty imposed on all who sin – death. He earned forgiveness for all who believe."

One special convert was a man named Jason. He not only believed, but offered his house as our residence. Our preaching continued to prove fruitful – and resulted in a problem. Many of the synagogue's leading women and a large group of Greek proselytes became believers, splitting the congregation in two. Those who refused to believe became angry and determined to stop us. Rumors were scattered among the city's populace spreading vicious lies about us such as, "These men have caused trouble everywhere! Their followers are breaking the laws of the Emperor, saying that there is another king, whose name is Jesus."

Our lives were threatened; we sought protection. A mob attacked Jason's house, looking for us. When it was determined that we could not be found, the mob turned to Jason and other believers who were there. Many of these, because of their faith, were deemed enemies of the state and imprisoned. They had to forfeit bail before being released. Fortunately, Silas, Timothy and I had been safely hidden in a neighboring house where we remained until night time. Our believing friends then helped us escape the city; sending us to Berea.

Berea proved a joy. My first synagogue sermon resulted in converts. The people were open to our message. They listened with eagerness; searching the Scriptures to validate what we taught. Many Greek men and women became believers.

But our euphoria did not last; unbelieving Thessalonian Jews arrived. Word had reached them of our success and they were determined to stop it. The same technique found successful in Thessalonica was used in Berea. These Judaizers stirred up the people, and that led to formation of an enraged mob. Our friends took no chances. I was sent away to Athens; Silas and Timothy stayed behind.

Athens proved a city of wonder: worshippers, debaters, and philosophers. As I waited for Silas and Timothy to join me, I had ample time to become acquainted with the city and its apparent passion for marble images of gods. Early in my stay I was able to find the city's only synagogue. It was there that I first presented the Good News. Later I learned that certain public squares were centers for intellectual debate. I visited several and shared my theological beliefs with those present. Among them were certain Epicurean and Stoic teachers.

I took pleasure in knowing that in these squares a person could present his philosophical position openly without fear of repercussion.

I must have evoked certain interest. I was noticed, but not always in a complimentary way. Some regarded me as an ignorant show-off. Others listening to my arguments about Jesus and the resurrection thought of me as preaching about foreign gods; a topic of interest.

I was invited to speak to the City Council in a square called the Areopagus. The Council's request, "We would like to know what this new teaching is that you are talking about. Some of the things we hear you say sound strange to us, and we would like to know what they mean." This audience was unique in character; highly intelligent and well educated. I attempted to speak to them at their level. My message can be summarized in these few words:

"I see that in every way you Athenians are very religious. For as I walked through your city and looked at the places where you worship, I found an altar on which is written, 'To an Unknown God.' That which you worship, then, even though you do not know it, is what I proclaim to you. The God who made the world and everything in it is the Lord of heaven and earth and does not live in man-made temples. Nor does he need anything that we can supply by working for him, since it is he himself who gives life and breath and everything else to everyone. From one man he created all races of mankind and made them live throughout the whole earth. He himself fixed beforehand the exact times and the limits of the places where they would live. He did this so that they would look for him, and perhaps find him as they felt around for him. Yet God is actually not far from any one of us; as someone has said, 'In him we live and move and exist.'

"It is as some of your poets have said, 'We too are his children.' Since we are God's children, we should not suppose that his nature is anything like an image of gold or silver or stone, shaped by the art and skill of man. God has overlooked the times when people did not know him, but now he commands all of them everywhere to turn away from their evil ways. For he has fixed a day in which he will judge the whole world with justice by means of a man he has chosen. He has given proof of this to everyone by raising that man from death."

My last comment, the one about raising Jesus from death, proved too much. Several began to heckle me; but not all. Some wanted to hear more. As I left, several followed. While the members of the synagogue and the vast majority of Council listeners gave little credence to my words, a few persons, including Dionysius, a member of the Council, and a woman named Damaris heeded my message and did become believers.

Soon after the Areopagus event, Silas and Timothy arrived. Further evangelizing in Athens seemed to bear little fruit. We decided on an alternate plan. I would explore new *territory* by going to Corinth, while my companions would return and strengthen the churches we had already begun. Timothy would return to Thessalonica, and after spending time with the Bereans, Silas would return to Philippi.

I found Corinth to be a cosmopolitan city with a sizable Jewish population. My prayer, "Heavenly Father, bless my work. Help me to successfully establish a sizeable following for your son."

✠ ✠ ✠

Paul in Thessalonica, Berea, and Athens: Acts 17:1-34

Then Priscilla Said

I am Priscilla, wife and partner of the tentmaker, Aquila. We are Christian Jews who migrated to Rome from the province of Pontus on the Black Sea. Jews were tolerated by the Roman government; granted protection under law. However, all that changed when unbelieving Jews in Rome began to persecute believing Jews. Believers were considered blasphemers. Homes were attacked; people were killed . . . all in the name of Yahweh. Such behavior soon reached the ears of Emperor Claudius. It could not be allowed within his capital. Roman toleration ceased. The emperor cared little about the reason for the trouble, and even less about who the guilty parties were. He knew they were Jews; they had upset the *status quo* and that was enough. As a result, all Jews were uprooted from their homes and banished from Rome, the innocent along with the guilty.

We chose Corinth, the capital of the Roman province of Achaia and a trade city strategically located on that narrow isthmus separating the northern Corinthian Gulf from the southern Saronic Gulf that bordered the peninsula. A stone tramway transversed the isthmus allowing ships and their cargos to be transported across, dragging them from shore to shore. This practice permitted traders to shorten their journey and avoid the often-stormy waters off southern Achaia.

Corinth had a broad based ethnic population that included traders from distant lands. We would fit right in; and we were not alone. Other Christians who had fled Rome became our friends. We would worship in each other's homes, away from critical eyes.

However, we soon learned of the religious underside to the city. It was a religious center devoted to the many gods of Rome. But even more, the city contained at least twelve temples, many on the acropolis fortress jutting high above and to the south of the city; its most infamous temple dedicated to the Greek goddess of love, Aphrodite. Here, temple priestesses practiced religious prostitution with worshipers.

Immediately upon our arrival in Corinth, we searched the marketplace, found a small open-air shop to rent, and proceeded to set up our tent-making business. We had chosen wisely. Our business grew. We soon found need for an assistant. That's when our new friend, another Jewish tentmaker by the name of Paul, arrived in town. He claimed to be an evangelistic crusader for our Lord Jesus Christ and needed work to sustain his missionary efforts. Paul proved to be an accomplished tent maker as well as a true Christian man – God was good. Lodging and board would be included as part of our collaborative agreement. Our attraction to him was instantaneous; the beginning of a deep and lasting friendship. His enthusiastic love for his Savior proved contagious; infectious. And he proved to be an excellent teacher. Many of our faith questions were answered.

✠ ✠ ✠

Work days were devoted to tent-making, but on each Sabbath Paul could be found at the local synagogue in earnest discussion, seeking to convince both the Jews and proselyte Greeks present that Jesus is the Messiah promised in the Scriptures. Paul's routine changed when his companions Silas and Timothy arrived from Macedonia. As previously agreed, he now excused himself from our business. He would devote all energy to his life's task, teaching about Jesus. His companion's report on the situation in Thessalonica persuaded him to write the believers, encouraging them in their faith. The letter finished, Paul's time was now devoted to preaching in the streets and the synagogue the Good News that Jesus is the Messiah; but his efforts produced little reward. Few believed. After continuous opposition from the traditional Jews and proselyte Greeks, he protested his disgust by shaking the dust from his clothes and saying to them, "If you are lost, you yourselves must take the blame for it. I am not responsible. From now on I will go to the Gentiles." And so he did.

Titius Justus, a proselyte Greek who lived next door to the synagogue, did believe. He invited Paul, Silas, and Timothy to accept room and board at his house. The three men's missionary efforts outside the synagogue proved highly successful. Crispus, who had been the leader of the synagogue, left the Jewish tradition and became a believer. He, all his family, and many other residents of Corinth heard the Good News message, believed, and were baptized. The Church was growing.

Paul came to visit us often; one time with a message – from *heaven*. He reported, "I just had to come and tell you. You are my dear friends. Last night I had a vision from God. He said to me, 'Do not be afraid, but keep on speaking and do not give up, for I am with you. No one will be able to harm you, for many in this city are my people.'" That was wonderful news. We believers were excited. Paul stayed with us for two and one-half years. – However, times of wonderful news do have limits.

It wasn't long before, once more, Paul was in trouble; attacked by his Jewish rivals. Aquila and I were finishing work on a

Bedouin tent when Timothy came running and shouting, "They seized Paul! They are taking him to the Praetorium. They will accuse him of promoting an illegal religion! A group of them are – right now – dragging him before the new proconsul, Gallio. He just recently arrived from the Delphi area, and has announced that he is available to hear litigation."

We arrived at the judgment hall just as the accusation against Paul was being pronounced; promoting an illegal religion. There on the blue and white platform, the marble *bema*, stood the leader of the Synagogue, Sosthenes. His accusation, "This man is trying to persuade people to worship God in a way that is against our law! He is preaching a doctrine that claims a rabbi has risen from the dead and is the Jewish Messiah. That message is contrary to our Law and opposed to historical Judaism; it cannot be tolerated in our religion. This Paul is preaching a new, unapproved religion, and only religions approved by the Senate are permissible in Caesar's empire!"

Paul struggled free and was about to speak when Gallio interrupted. "When I see Jews opposing Jews, I am reminded that not many years past Emperor Claudius rid Rome of all Jews, not because of their interpretation of religious law, but rather because of their violent behavior. Interpretation of Jewish law is not an area of my responsibility. If this were a matter of some evil crime or wrong that has been committed, it would be reasonable for me to be patient with you Jews; listen to your complaints and rule. But since it is an argument about words and names and your own law, you yourselves must settle it. I will not be the judge of such things!" With that, Gallio angrily ordered the Jews out of his court. The crowd that had gathered to listen near the court entrance took this as opportunity to express their disgust with the local Jewish population. Some rogues grabbed Sosthenes and beat him right in front of the Pretorium. Gallio was informed, but did not seem to care.

Gallio's ruling set a standard for future litigation. By refusing to pronounce judgment and dismissing the case as not applicable to Roman law, Gallio provided legal precedent for future Roman magistrates to apply when confronted with similar cases. We were ecstatic to hear Gallio's ruling; it gave Paul and his companions the legal right under Roman law to continue their apostolic mission. This right they employed to maximum ability. It also encouraged us to be more proactive as Christians. Erastus, Corinth's city treasurer, became a believer; not only a believer, but an active evangelist. He became a member of the group of missionaries surrounding Paul. The wealth he had generously used to build a pavement square in front of the city's theater would now be used to support the Lord's ministry.

It was during this same time that Aquila and I felt a significantly strong growth in faith and commitment. We became convinced that our future life's mission was to become crusaders for Christ. When the time came for Paul to move on, Aquila and I determined to join him. At Cenchreae, Paul committed to a Nazarite vow as an act of thanksgiving for the blessings God bestowed in Corinth. Enforcement of the vow began immediately after Paul shaved his head; for all the rules germane to a Nazarite, including letting his hair grow uncut, would be observed. We left Canchreae and sailed for Syria, with a stop at Ephesus. Paul used the stop as an opportunity to share the Good News. There were difficulties with the Jews and the Ephesian Christians needed guidance. Aquila and I felt God's call to stay. We could provide guidance and steadfastness. Paul would continue to Jerusalem and complete his vow.

Paul in Corinth: Acts 18:1-23
Nazarite vow: Numbers 6:1-21

Then Apollos Said

I am Apollos, a shortened version of the Greek name, Apollonius. I am an Egyptian Jew raised in the Hellenistic culture adopted by my country following Alexander the Great's conquest. But I am a believer; a Jewish Christian from Alexandria who repented and was baptized by John the Baptizer in the Jordan River. Then, on the Feast of Harvest, or as some say, Pentecost, I became one of three thousand believers in Jesus our Messiah. You see, when I was still a young man, I chose to leave my studies in Alexandria and follow the path of a scholar of Holy Scripture in Israel. It was here that I met John and was baptized; and it was here that I learned about my Messiah. Shortly after my conversion I returned to Egypt as one of many ambassadors for Christ.

There is a proud heritage of Judaism in Egypt. It was my ancestors who produced the Septuagint, that respected Greek translation of Holy Scripture. Tradition tells us that Ptolemy II once gathered 72 Jewish elders and placed them in 72 chambers, each in a separate one, without revealing to them why they were summoned. He entered each scholar's room and said: "Write for me the Torah of Moses, your teacher." Yahweh protected his holy writings from error; he put it in the heart of each man to translate identically as all the others did.

I am a product of what is sometimes call Hellenistic Judaism. I've studied Holy Scripture with an intense interest since my youth; putting many scrolls to memory. When I became a believer I found that knowledge a valuable force to convince my hearers that Jesus of Nazareth is the promised Messiah arisen from the dead.

I left my native country, Egypt, and sailed to Ephesus where I continued evangelizing for my Lord. The work has been satisfying; many converts. People seem eager to accept my message; many baptisms.

I met Aquila and Pricilla early after my arrival. They, as did I, were often found in the synagogue preaching and teaching the Good News. They were present when I baptized several new converts. As each new believer came forward I asked, "Are you ready to commit your life to service in Christ's kingdom?" Following a word of assent, I slowly lowered the person, just enough to cover the head, as I spoke the words taught by Brother John: "May this water be to you a cleansing of all sin; and may your pledge to live a righteous life be fulfilled through your action as God gives you the strength. Prepare the way of the Lord!"

Following the rite, Aquila and Pricilla invited me to their home where they approached me with this advice. "Apollos, allow us to offer guidance toward a more acceptable baptism rite. As you immersed the believer, you used words spoken by John the Baptizer before our Lord began his ministry. Those words no longer apply. John's baptism was for those who turned from their sins; for those who were preparing themselves to be believers in the one coming after him – that is, in Jesus. But now that Jesus has suffered, died, and risen from death, thus fulfilling his earthly ministry, one is to be baptized in his name." Their council was taken and greatly appreciated.

Since there was sufficient spiritual leadership in Ephesus, I offered to travel to Corinth and work there. My friends applauded the idea and wrote a letter to the believers asking that they welcome me. God blessed my efforts. Through convincing argument I was able to defeat the Jews in public debates by proving from the Scriptures that Jesus is the Messiah.

Sometime later I was told that a clarification similar to that offered me by Aquila and Pricilla was offered by Paul after he arrived in Ephesus. When Paul asked a group of disciples, "Did you receive the Holy Spirit when you believed?" they answered, "We have not even heard that there is a Holy Spirit." Paul's question, "Well, then, what kind of baptism did you receive?" Their response, "The baptism of John." Paul then instructed the believers as Aquila and Pricilla had instructed me. Following their re-baptizing in the name of the Lord Jesus, Paul placed his hands on them. What followed was forever regarded as a euphoric experience; the Holy Spirit came upon them and they spoke in strange tongues; just as had happened at Pentecost years previous.

✠ ✠ ✠

Apollos: Acts 18:24-19:10

Then Demetrius Said

I am Demetrius, an Ephesian master silversmith and warden of the temple of Artemis; and I am angry! My business and that of my fellow craftsmen has fallen to a level that will force many of us to close our shops. – And all because of one man. We almost had him stopped; but he got away! And now our craft and our livelihood are threatened.

Ephesus is a port city of considerable repute; one of the largest in the empire. It is known throughout the Roman world as the home of Artemis, or as the Romans would say, Diana. She is the daughter of Zeus and Leto and the twin sister of Apollo. Her temple is here; the largest marble structure in the entire Greek world, in where she stands erect, proudly displaying her many breasts. She is worshipped as our mother goddess; goddess of childbirth, virginity and young girls, bringing and relieving disease in women. Great festivals are held in her honor. In one, young girls who reached puberty are initiated into her cult; they are asked to lay in front of the altar all the paraphernalia of their virginity, toys, dolls and locks of hair; thus preparing to leave the domain of virgin.

This man, this Paul who ruined our lives, is a Jew; but not the traditional Jew. Rather one that makes claim to an *arisen-from-the-dead* man who is now a god. We can easily tolerate a new god; we have many, but we cannot accept a deity whose very existence challenges the legitimacy of our great Artemis, and with it, the silversmith craft.

Several silversmiths expressed concern to me, "If all the people become Christians, to whom are we to sell our statues and statuettes? Those of *The Way* have no need for an Artemis shrine in their home. Why would anyone want an image of Artemis to pray to if this other god can do more; as they maintain, much more?"

Another said, "This Paul claims that we should worship his Father God and the risen son, Jesus Christ; the one he calls Messiah. He preaches a message that alleges this Jesus came down from heaven to live a perfect life in our stead, to suffer and die on a Roman cross for our sins, and then to rise from death three days later. He then asserts that this Jesus is now in heaven ruling over everything; the whole world. His bottom line is: believe my message and you are guaranteed heaven. His message was reinforced with what appeared to be miracles; driving out evil spirits and healing illness. Even handkerchiefs and aprons Paul had used were taken for healing to the sick."

Seven sons of a Jewish High Priest named Sceva, men who had a reputation for using magic to drive away evil spirits, tried to use Paul's *Jesus power* as magic to cast out an evil spirit from a man who was violent. I was there; I saw it. These sons approached the possessed man's house. They stopped several paces before the door and called for the man to come out. The door opened. A creature with a ghastly appearance came forward. The sons instinctively took a step back, but they did not retreat. Standing fast, they, as one, challenged the evil spirit with these words, "I command you in the name of Jesus, whom Paul preaches, to go out of this man!" The evil spirit responded, "I know Jesus and I know about Paul; but you – who are you?" With that, this possessed creature sprang forward and attacked the sons with such a violence that he defeated them, wounding them and forcing them to flee with much of their clothes torn off.

News of this event spread like wild fire. Many feared Paul's *Jesus power.* Believers came, publicly admitting their former practice of magic. A bonfire was lit; magic books were brought and thrown into the fire; their worth exceeding thousands of denarii.

Because of Paul, scores of Ephesians have believed and joined what was called *The Way* of the Lord. Because of Paul, the *bottom fell out* of our business. We were desperate. Paul needed to be stopped.

✠ ✠ ✠

I called for a meeting of all the master craftsmen and others whose livelihood was dependent on temple worship. It would take place in the Temple of Artemis the following morning. We were over one hundred persons. When all had gathered I announced, "Men, you know that our prosperity comes from this work. You can see and hear for yourselves what this fellow Paul is doing. He says that gods made by men are not gods at all, and has succeeded in convincing many people, both here in Ephesus and in nearly the whole province of Asia. There is danger, then, that this business of ours will get a bad name. Not only that, there is also the danger that the temple of the great goddess Artemis will come to mean nothing and that her greatness will be destroyed – the goddess worshipped by everyone in Asia and in the entire world!"

Demetrius the silversmith

My appeal began to produce its desired reaction. Resentment grew. I warned, "Your livelihoods would be lost!" I could see rage in the eyes of many. "Your wives and children will lack food!" Anger intensified. "You will not be able to clothe them!" – That was enough. – Someone shouted, "Great is Artemis of Ephesus!" The crowd's ferocity grew in intensity. There were more shouts, "Great is Artemis of Ephesus!" Soon the temple was filled with a unified cadence, "Great is Artemis of Ephesus! Great is Artemis of Ephesus!" A parade began to form. Several took leadership. They marched out of the temple past the Prytanium and on to Curetes Street, and then turned at the Celsus Library into Marble Street, still shouting in tempo the greatness of Artemis. The procession had doubled in size. I had done my job well.

Two of Paul's men, Gaius and Aristarchus, happened to be on Marble Street. They were grabbed and forced to march. Other Jews were required to join. The procession continued to grow as it moved into the theater. Once in the theater, bedlam held sway. Many had no idea why they were there. Everyone was shouting; some one thing, others another.

Those Jews forced to join the parade were manhandled to the stage. Alexander, a prominent Jew of *The Way* was forced to the front. He motioned with his hand for quiet. As he began to speak a shout was heard, "This man is a Jew. Don't listen to him!" Again the chant began, first by a band to the left of the stage, but quickly stretching around to the right, all shouting, "Great is Artemis of Ephesus!"

This chaos continued until the City Clerk stepped forward. The clerk was recognized by all present as one who should be listened to and could be trusted to advise well. "Men of Ephesus, listen!" he beckoned." Everyone knows that the city of Ephesus is the keeper of the temple of the great Artemis and of the sacred stone that fell down from heaven. Nobody can deny these things. So then, you must calm down and not do anything reckless. You have brought these men here, even though they have not robbed temples or said evil things about our goddess. If Demetrius and his workers have an accusation

Ephesus theater
Wikipedia - rated public domain
File: Great Theater.jpg

against someone, there are the regular days of court and there are the authorities; they can accuse each other there. But if there is something more that you want, it will have to be settled in the legal meeting of citizens; for there is the danger that we will be accused of a riot in what has happened today. There is no excuse for all this uproar, and we would not be able to give a good reason for it."

The crowd was pacified, the theater emptied. Our cause would not be heard. Those of *The Way* had won for now.

✠ ✠ ✠

Paul in Ephesus: Acts 19:11-41

Then Silas Said

I am Silas, sometimes called Silvanus. I accompanied Paul during much of his missionary journey life. Our liaison began with a meeting. Upon return to Antioch in Syria, following Paul and Barnabas' missionary journey, it became necessary to travel to Jerusalem to confer with our brothers about whether or not obedience to the Mosaic Laws was required of Gentile believers. This particular concern centered on circumcision: "Did believing Gentiles need to be circumcised?" Our Council ruled that the Mosaic Laws directed to Jewish Christians should not be forced on Gentile Christians. Only a few select laws were required.

Sometime after returning to Antioch, Paul and Barnabas, his partner on their first journey, agreed to a second tour that would include re-visiting the towns they had previously evangelized. However, when Barnabas insisted that the young man Mark again join them, Paul refused. When it was determined that neither man would yield his will, they decided to undertake separate routes. Barnabas agreed to go back to Cyprus and take Mark with him. Paul chose to go through Syria and Cilicia with me as his partner.

We journeyed north and westward, crossing into Macedonia and on to Philippi, where after a fruitful stay, continued southward to Thessalonica, Berea, and Corinth. When, after a one and one-half year stay in Corinth, we returned to Jerusalem. Our journey ran full circle when we arrived back at Antioch.

Then, after spending some time in Antioch we again left, visiting the regions of Galatia and Phrygia, strengthening the believers; then trekking on to Ephesus. Our ministry here proved highly fruitful. A number of churches were established, witchcraft was weakened, and the worship of the goddess Artemis declined. We next revisited Macedonia and Greece, staying about three months. Paul then determined to return to Jerusalem for Pentecost. He, together with a number of fellow missionaries, departed Corinth.

Paul had originally intended to sail directly to Syria, but was forced to choose a land route through Macedonia because of a Jewish plot against him. As a result, the churches in Beria, Thessalonica, and Philippi again enjoyed our presence. After a short stay in Troas we arrived at Miletus for a final meeting with the church elders from Ephesus. Following a sad farewell, we sailed, passing through Tyre and Ptolemais to Caesarea. Our final destination would again be Jerusalem.

Review of 2nd and 3rd journeys: Acts 15-19
Returning to Jerusalem: Acts 20:1-21:16

Then Michael Said

I am Michael, Paul's fourteen year-old nephew. My father, my mother who is Paul's sister, and I live in Jerusalem. My father is a highly positioned Pharisee, a member of the Sanhedrin. He hates my uncle; considers him to be a blasphemer; one who abandoned the true Jewish faith for what is now called *The Way*.

✠ ✠ ✠

The whole family regards Paul as a humiliation. Grandfather is furious! "I was so proud of my son; he had been brought up in strict Judaic tradition, not as a Sadducee, but as a true Jew, a Pharisee. Our family has always been strongly Pharisaic. My son worked feverishly to destroy a new sect whose teaching proclaimed a Jesus of Nazareth was the promised Messiah. I supported his efforts. The Church regarded him as a leader; an ardent protector of our tradition.

"But then he broke my heart. He became a follower of the very sect he had been persecuting. My son, my blood, began to teach in the sacred synagogues that this Jesus suffered and died on a Roman cross to pay the penalty for all sin. And most blasphemous of all, he taught that this Jesus rose from death and now rules from heaven with Yahweh. My family is ashamed; my wife, my sons and daughters mortified.

"Then he did the outrageous – Paul began a ministry to Gentiles. He claimed that Gentiles were part of God's family through faith in this Jesus as Messiah; that obedience to the Torah was not required. What could I do? I could not tolerate such blasphemy. I disowned him. He is an apostate, a foe to God and the chosen race – and a disgrace to my family."

✠ ✠ ✠

I knew about Paul; after all, he is my uncle. – And I also knew about Jesus; he is my Savior. Yes, that's what I said, Jesus is my Savior. I had become a believer, a secret believer a short time ago. None of my family knows. No one knows. All thought I would follow in my family's footsteps and become a Pharisee like my father and my grandfather.

Probably because our family was a ranking Pharisaic family, I was allowed a fairly free reign within the Temple and Hall of Hewn Stone. I learned from various conversations that Uncle Paul was in Jerusalem. Rumor had it that he was here to report to James the Just and the elders of *The Way* the progress of his missionary outreach. We also heard rumors that he intended to support four men as they fulfilled their Temple rite, a necessary act to complete their Nazarite vow.

When I heard that the very next day Uncle Paul was going to be in the Temple, I made certain I was present also. I entered the Court of Women. There my uncle was with four men I didn't know. This is where the ceremony of purification with the four men would be to be initiated through a spiritual rite; and since Uncle Paul was known to have associated with Gentiles, I assumed the elders of *The Way* had thought it best that Paul purify himself along with the men. I think that this was done so that Jews in general might see that Uncle was observing the Mosaic Law.

I watched as my uncle approached a kiosk dedicated to

Nazarites. I could hear Paul as he spoke to the priest, "I have been away from the holy city for some time and have had intimate dealings with Gentiles. I would like to submit to the rite of purification. I wish to be spiritually purified, for it is my intention to support these four impoverished men who are with me by providing the funds for the offerings required to complete their Nazarite vows."

The priest directed, "You are acting wisely. You must first regain ceremonial purity for yourself. You can do this through the seven-day Ritual of Purification. When the purification is complete you may then accompany these four Jewish men in the absolution ceremony. We will set up a purification schedule. You must return to the Temple on agreed regular intervals during this week for the appropriate rites. Part of the ritual will include a sprinkling with Water of Atonement on the third and seventh days."

I returned each day to watch. On the third day Paul recognized me. We hugged; I told him my secret; he assured me it would be kept. When the seventh day, the day of purification finally arrived, the priest who had been supervising the rite led my uncle and the four men into the Court of Israel. I *tagged* along. Paul had purchased the required offerings to the Lord. – I had memorized that requirement in Hebrew School. It included: one male lamb in its first year without blemish as a burnt offering, one ewe lamb in its first year without blemish as a sin offering, one ram without blemish boiled as a peace offering, a basket of unleavened bread, cakes of fine flour mixed with oil, unleavened wafers anointed with oil, and a grain offering with its drink offerings.

I continued to watch as several Levites brought all of the offerings to the Court of the Priests and carried them before the Lord's Altar. One by one the sacrifices were placed upon the Altar. A Levite presented the male lamb to the presiding priest. After a careful examination, the priest placed his hands on its head to signify the transfer of guilt and the animal was then slaughtered as the persons' substitute. Blood was collected with a portion sprinkled against the Altar. Finally, the entire skinned carcass of the animal was totally consumed by fire.

The blood of the ewe lamb was the main feature of the sin offering. Once the blood was drained from the animal, the priest sprinkled it on the Altar a total of seven times. – All Jews are taught at an early age to honor the number seven; it symbolizes completeness; in this case, total absolution of sin. Then the fatty tissues were collected and burned on the Altar. Finally, Levites collected the remaining parts of the animal and burned them at the rear of the Altar. The last offering was the peace offering. A ram was forced before the Altar. The four men placed their hands on the ram's head. They then stood in a semicircle around the ram and at signal a priest slit its throat. Blood gushed out in a steady stream into a vessel held by the priest. The priest then sprinkled all four sides of the Altar. The ram was gutted, skinned, cut in sections, placed into a vessel of water, and boiled over the Altar; parts were burned. After completing this last animal sacrifice, a basket of unleavened bread, the grain offering, and the drink offering were set before the Altar.

That deed signaled a final action. All watched as the four Nazarites stepped to the balustrade separating the two courts. With Levites assisting, each man shaved his head, collecting every hair. The priest then took the hair from the consecrated heads and put it on the fire which was under the sacrifice of the peace offering.

The priests next took a boiled shoulder of the ram, one unleavened cake from the basket, one unleavened wafer, and put each upon the clasped hands of the four Nazarites. They next removed each offering and raised it above their heads as a wave offering before the Lord. This together with the ram's breast as a wave offering and the thigh of the heave offering became food holy for the priest. When the ritual was complete, all participants were told to wait until ushered to a secluded area within the Women's Court for a communal meal; the former Nazarites were to again taste wine.

It was then, while arrangements were being made, that my uncle's world came apart! A band of zealots broke into the meal area and grabbed my uncle, dragging him out through the Beautiful Gate of the Women's Court and into the Court of Gentiles, all the time shouting, "Help! This is the man who goes everywhere teaching everyone against the people of Israel, the Law of Moses, and this Temple. And now he has even brought some Gentiles into the Temple and defiled this holy place!" One of the group added, "He was seen bringing a Gentile into the Women's Court to defile it. He deserves to die!"

I was terrified for my uncle. Everyone knew that there were signs before every entrance to the Court of Women with this stern warning:

> "No Gentile may enter beyond the dividing wall into the court around the holy place; whoever is caught will be to blame for his subsequent death."

What would happen to Uncle?

All worshippers were forced out of the Women's Court and its doors closed. As Uncle was being pulled and pushed through the Court of Gentiles a mob began to form; they struck him with fists. Uncle Paul was beaten to his knees and may have been killed, except that the regimental Roman commander and his troops appeared from a subterranean passageway. They raced into the courtyard with spears in thrust position.

The mob stopped beating Uncle and cowered from the soldiers. Uncle Paul was arrested and tied with chains to his arms and legs. The commander motioned for quiet, "Who is this man, and what has he done?" There was no clear answer. The commander ordered Uncle taken to the Antonio Fortress. The crowd protested, again trying to beat my uncle. "Kill him!" they cried. Finally, the soldiers grabbed Uncle and physically carried him out of the Temple and up the steps to the Fortress.

My uncle was about to be led into the fortress when I saw him call to the commander. I worked my way to the front of the mob. Uncle yelled at the commander, "May I say something to you?" The commander seemed startled. "Do you speak Greek? Then you are not that Egyptian fellow who some time ago started a revolution and led four thousand armed terrorist out into the desert?" Uncle answered, "I am a Jew, born in Tarsus of Cilicia, a citizen of an important city. Please let me speak to the people." Permission was granted. Uncle stood on the steps and motioned with his hands to the mob. When they were quiet, he spoke to them, not in Greek, but this time in Hebrew. I distinctly remember how he began:

"Men, brothers, and fathers, listen to me as I make my defense before you. I am a Jew, born in Tarsus of Cilicia, but brought up here in Jerusalem as a student of Gamaliel." Then he went on telling how he had persecuted those of *The Way*. How, when commissioned by the High Priest and the Sanhedrin, went to Damascus to arrest Jesus believers.

He then announced, "As I was traveling and coming near Damascus, about midday a bright light from the sky flashed suddenly around. I fell to the ground and heard a voice saying to me, 'Saul, Saul! Why do you persecute me?'" Uncle next exclaimed how the light had blinded him and how a man named Ananias healed his vision and counseled him. He said that this miraculous experience had convinced him that Jesus of Nazareth was the Messiah all Jews had been waiting for. He even announced that he was baptized in the name of Jesus for the forgiveness of his sins.

Paul taken prisoner at the Jerusalem temple

Then he went on to report, "When I returned to Jerusalem, and while I was praying in the Temple I had a vision. I was told by Jesus that I was to be a missionary to the Gentiles."

The mob had been patient, but that reference to the Gentiles set them off. They shouted, "Away with him! Kill him! He's not fit to live!" They screamed; they waved clothing; they threw dust in the air. A full riot broke out; Uncle's safety was threatened. He had to be taken inside the fortress. I hoped his Roman citizenship would help him there.

✝ ✝ ✝

I was in the Hall of Hewn Stones when the very next day Uncle Paul was brought by soldiers to the Council for questioning. His defense was brilliant. As soon as he realized that the Council was made up of Pharisees and Sadducees, he began to shout, "My brothers! I am a Pharisee, the son of Pharisees! I am on trial here because I hope that the dead will rise to life!" That did it. – A vehement quarrel ensured; one group shouting against the other group. When one party yelled, "We cannot find a thing wrong with this man! Perhaps a spirit or an angel really did speak to him!" it got so bad in the chamber that a near riot broke out. The soldiers removed Paul and led him under guard back to the barracks. I trailed behind.

I later returned to the Hall of Hewn Stone. About forty zealot Jews were meeting and planning. I heard one say, "We must kill this deceiver, Paul. I vow that I will not eat or drink anything until Paul is dead. Who is with me?" A resounding consensus rang throughout the hall.

The men proceeded to the Council Chambers and presented their plan. Leading members of the Sanhedrin were to request of the Roman commander a second hearing. These zealots would secretly position themselves along the street leading from the fortress to the Council Chambers. Paul would be struck down before he reached the chambers. – I couldn't let that happen.

I needed a chance to talk with my uncle. I knew what to do; I would bring him food. A local shop sold me a small skin of wine, a loaf of wheat bread, figs, and an apple. With my meal in hand I approached the fortress and requested if I might bring my uncle some food and visit him in his prison cell. The request was quickly granted. I followed the guard down steps to the dungeon below. As I arrived in the cell area, I could see Paul sitting on a stool with his head bowed. I called, "Uncle Paul, I've come to visit you. And I've brought you some food." He immediately stood up and smiled. The iron gate was opened and I entered. The guard shut it and left.

Paul was hungry; prison food was only gruel and water. We talked, but I was scared; there was real danger. I looked about; no one was near. I whispered, "Uncle Paul, you are in grave danger. Tomorrow the High Priest will again request that you be brought before the Council for further questioning. The request is a ruse. While guards lead you from the fort to the Hall of Hewn Stone, a group of forty zealots will be secretly hiding, and as you pass they will attack and kill you. These men are very determined. They have vowed not to eat until you are dead."

Paul showed no fear. Only mumbled, "God will deal with this also." He then called for the guard and requested, "Please take this lad to your commander; he has something to tell him that is of great importance." I kissed my uncle goodbye and followed the guard. We entered the commander's quarters. The guard stopped at attention and reported, "Sir, the prisoner Paul called and asked me to bring this young man to you because he has something to say to you." The guard was dismissed and I was led off to a secluded area. "What do you have to tell me, son?" I told the commander everything I knew about the assassination plan. "The Jewish authorities have agreed to ask you tomorrow to take Paul down to the Council Hall, pretending that the Council wants to get more accurate information about him. But don't listen to them, because there are more than forty men who will be hiding and waiting for him. They have taken a vow not to eat or drink until they kill him. They are now ready to do it, and are waiting for your decision." The commander looked directly into my eyes and demanded, "Don't tell anyone that you have reported this to me." Then he escorted me out of the fortress. I told no one.

I learned later that Paul had been escorted under guard out of Jerusalem at night and was being held in a Caesarea Maritima prison under the jurisdiction of Governor Felix.

Paul's visit to Jerusalem: Acts 21:17-23:24
Temple sacrifices: Leviticus 1, 2, 3, 4
Rules for a Nazarite: Numbers 6:1-21

Then Governor Felix Said

I am Antonius Felix, governor of Judea. My name means fortunate and that is true. I am a freedman, a former slave. It helped that my brother Pallas was secretary of the Roman treasury. My wife is the Judean princess, Drusilla, daughter of Herod Agrippa I, king over the territory once ruled by his great grandfather Herod the Great. I was governor when Paul was brought under guard from Jerusalem.

I received this letter from Commander Lysias:

"Claudius Lysias to his Excellency, the Governor Felix: Greetings.

> The Jews seized this man and were about to kill him. I learned that he is a Roman citizen, so I went with my soldiers and rescued him. I wanted to know what they were accusing him of, so I took him down to their Council. I found out that he had not done a thing for which he deserved to die or be put in prison; the accusation against him had to do with questions about their own law. And when I was informed that some Jews were making a plot against him I decided to

send him to you. I told his accusers to make their charges against him before you."

After reading the letter and questioning the prisoner briefly, I had him held under guard in Herod's palace. As expected, five days later I was visited by some of the Jewish elders and a lawyer named Tertullus. I arranged a hearing. When all were present, I inquired about the accusation. This fellow Tertullus spoke, and as usual, began with flattery. "Your Excellency! Your wise leadership has brought a long period of peace, and many necessary reforms are being made for the good of our country." . . . And so he continued, finally getting to the point which turned out to be: "This Paul is a dangerous nuisance; he starts riots among the Jews all over the world; he is a leader of a party of the Nazarenes; he defiled the temple."

That was that. Now I motioned Paul to defend himself. He also began with flattery; but it was short. "I know that you have been a judge over this nation for many years, and so I am happy to defend myself before you." His defense was basically a denial of all accusations: "I just arrived in Jerusalem twelve days ago; I was not arguing or stirring up trouble; and they provide no proof of their accusations."

Then Paul changed his tactic. "I do admit this to you: I worship the God of our ancestors by following *The Way* which they say is false. But I also believe in all the things written in the Law of Moses and the books of the prophets. I have the same hope in God that these themselves hold, that all men, both the good and the bad, will raise from death. And so I do my best always to have a clear conscience before God and men."

Then Paul went on to explain that he had been away from Jerusalem and had returned with an offering to aid the poor of his church and offer sacrifices. He then asserted, "It was while I was doing this that they found me in the Temple, after

I had completed the Ceremony of Purification. There was no crowd with me, and no disorder." He then asked where those who originally arrested him were. "They should be here to accuse me." He ended his defense with these words: "I am being judged by you today for believing that the dead will rise to life."

Paul defends himself before Felix
Wikipedia: William Hogarth, Rated as public domain
File: Paul before Felix.jpg

That was enough. I knew about *The Way*. My wife was Jewish; a well informed Jewess. I announced, "The hearing is closed.

I will decide your case when the commander Lysias arrives. Guard, keep this prisoner under your care, but give him some freedom and allow his friends to provide for his needs. You are dismissed."

I found it helpful to have Paul meet with me and my wife Drusilla. She was very interested in his message. Paul talked with us about faith in Christ Jesus. He often made me feel uncomfortable with his talk about goodness, self-control, and especially the coming Day of Judgment. Some of what he said scared me.

I suppose I should have freed him, but I thought that with enough time there might be a supporter of Paul who had *get-out-of-jail* money to share. Two years passed and none came. My term as governor ended. Porcius Festus took my office and Paul remained in prison.

✠ ✠ ✠

Paul before Governor Felix: Acts 23:33-24:25

Then Governor Festus Said

I am Antonius Festus, sent by Caesar Nero to be the eleventh Roman governor of Judea. Felix had left with many problems unsolved. I was appointed to solve them; to put an end to uncontrollable crime, and crush the Jewish bands of *Sicarii* who opposed the government through political assassinations. – I also discovered that Felix had failed to deal with one of his famous prisoners. His name was Paul.

Resolution of Paul's situation was required. Three days after arriving in Caesarea, I found it necessary to visit my most important Jewish city, Jerusalem. On the very day of my arrival I was approached by the chief priests and Jewish leaders. Their singular concern, stop Paul. They insisted I do them a favor; have Paul brought to Jerusalem for trial. I would not submit to their scheme. My response, "Paul is being kept a prisoner in Caesarea, and I myself will be going back there soon. Let your leaders go to Caesarea with me and accuse the man, if he has done anything wrong."

I remained in Jerusalem for more than a week enjoying the luxury of Herod's Palace. During that time it became obvious what the concern of the Jewish leadership was. I learned of events that went back to a particular Pentecost Sunday many years past. It was on that day that a new Jewish cult was launched. It grew quickly into a sizable force. Three of the leaders were men named James the Just, Peter, and John. This group was bitterly opposed by the traditional Jewish leadership. My prisoner, Paul, until his conversion to the cult's faith, was a leading protagonist against the group, persecuting the believers. In spite of a constant threat, this Jewish cult was now organized into a strong and growing religious body. The Jewish Council was losing control of the masses.

The day after my return to Caesarea I sat down in the judgment court and ordered Paul to be brought in. He appeared to be a man of character. I called for quiet and ordered that those pressing charges against Paul speak. It soon became obvious that none of the accusations could be proven, nor were they the concern of a Roman court. Paul's defense was direct. "I have done nothing wrong against the Law of the Jews, or the Temple, or the Roman Emperor."

While I concurred with Paul's reasoning, I had to deal with the political aspects of this hearing. It would not be wise to simply dismiss the case and free Paul. I had to show some support to those who came all the way from Jerusalem. My response could affect my future. I could not appear to be anti-Jewish. I intended to have a positive relationship with the Council. Perhaps a change of venue would demonstrate my good will. I asked Paul, "Would you be willing to go to Jerusalem and be tried on these charges before me there?" Paul's response was immediate, "I am standing before the Emperor's own judgment court, where I should be tried. I have done no wrong to the Jews, as you yourself well know. If I have broken the law and done something for which I deserve the death penalty, I do not ask to escape it. But if there is no truth in the charges they bring against me, no one can hand me over to them. I appeal to the Emperor."

I did not expect this response. I emptied the court room and conferred with my advisors. Following their counsel, I ordered the parties back to the court. Then, to assure clarity, I asked. "Paul, you have publicly expressed every Roman citizen's right; the right to appeal your case before Caesar. Do you stand by that appeal?" Paul's response, "I do." " Alright then, this is my ruling: Paul, you have appealed to the Emperor; to the Emperor you will go."

✠ ✠ ✠

Sometime later I was visited by King Agrippa II and his sister Bernice. I did my best to entertain them and make them *feel at home*. As I shared the benefits and concerns associated with my office, the matter of Paul's trial came up. I explained that he remained a prisoner when Felix left office, even though he had been held for years accused but not convicted. I also explained the circumstances surrounding this latest confrontation with Jewish emissaries from Jerusalem. I related, "His opponents stood up, but they did not accuse him of any of the evil crimes that I thought they would. All they had were some arguments with him about their own religion and about a man named Jesus, who has died; but Paul claims that he is alive." Then I continued, "I was undecided about how I could get information on these matters, so I asked Paul if he would be willing to go to Jerusalem and be tried there on these charges. But Paul appealed; he asked to be kept under guard and let the Emperor decide his case. So I gave orders for him to be kept under guard until I could send him to Nero." Agrippa was interested; he suggested, "I would like to hear this man myself."

My next move had been anticipated earlier. A grand introduction to Agrippa and Bernice was already in the plans for the very next day. Paul would be part of the entertainment. The great and the powerful had already been invited. It would be a grand affair held in the Audience Hall of the Palace, a glorious space, by the harbor, its walls enclosing an ornate geometric mosaic floor. Agrippa and Bernice arrived with great pomp and ceremony. They entered the hall with the military chiefs and the leading men of the city, each seated at assigned couches. After proper introductions and a receptive acceptance, a festive meal was served to all; each course accompanied with performers, singing and dancing. After an appropriate respite to settle the meal, Paul was brought before the assembly.

I stood before the assembly to announce and explain. "King Agrippa, and all who are here with us: You see this man against whom all the Jewish people, both here and in Jerusalem, have brought complaints to me. They contend that he should not live any longer. But I could not find that he had done anything for which he deserved the death sentence. And since he himself made an appeal to the Emperor, I have decided to send him. But I do not have anything definite about him to write to the Emperor. So I have brought him here before this assembly – and especially before you, King Agrippa – so that, after investigating his case, I may have something to write. For it seems unreasonable to me to send a prisoner without clearly indicating the charges against him." At that point Agrippa spoke to Paul, "You have permission to speak on your own behalf."

Paul seemed pleased to be able to defend himself before the king. He spoke with confidence when he claimed that Agrippa knew and understood Jewish tradition. After asking the king to listen to his defense with patience, Paul began to review his life as a Jew and as Pharisee; how he persecuted those who became Christians. He again reviewed the revealing event while on the way to Damascus; the bright light, and the voice calling, "Saul, Saul! Why are you persecuting me?" Paul claimed the voice of that of Jesus of Nazareth.

"King Agrippa, this is what Jesus said to me, 'I have appeared to you to appoint you as my servant; you are to tell others what you have seen of me today, and what I will show you in the future. I will save you from the people of Israel and from the Gentiles, to whom I will send you. You are to open their eyes and turn them from darkness to the light, and from the power of Satan to God, so that through their faith in my redemptive action, they will have their sins forgiven and receive their place among God's chosen people.'"

Paul then confirmed that from the time of that miracle he had become a disciple of Jesus, preaching to both Jews and Gentiles that they must repent of their sins, turn to God, and do the things that would show they have repented. He then proclaimed, "This is the reason that the Jews seized me while I was in the temple, and tried to kill me. But I have been saved by God. – What I say is the very same thing the prophets and Moses said was going to happen: that the Messiah must suffer and be the first one to rise from death, to announce the light of salvation to the Jews and to the Gentiles."

That last was too much. I shouted at him, "You are mad, Paul! Your great learning is driving you mad!" Paul answered, "I am not mad, your Excellency! The words I speak are true and sober."

Then he switched his focus to my guest. "King Agrippa! I can speak to you with all boldness, because you know about these things. I am sure that you have taken notice of every one of them, for this thing has not happened hidden away in a corner. King Agrippa, do you believe the prophets? I know that you do!"

Agrippa was taken aback. "In this short time do you think you will make me a Christian?" Paul's response, "Whether a short time or a long time, my prayer to God is that you and all the rest who are listening to me today might become what I am – except, of course, for these chains!" With that, Paul was ushered out and the assembly departed. The king, Bernice, and I agreed, "This man has not done anything for which he should die or be put in prison." Agrippa's final words, "This man could have been released if he had not appealed to the Emperor."

Paul before Festus and Agrippa: Acts 25:1-26:32

Then Julius Said

I am Julius, an officer of the Roman army contingent called *The Emperor's Regiment*. Our troops have the high honor of acting on command of the Emperor or those who are his client kings; men such as Agrippa II. My assignment was to deliver a man named Paul and several other prisoners to Emperor Nero in Rome.

Sailing with us were several of Paul's companions: Aristarchus from Thessalonica; Luke, a physician from Troas; and Timothy, a student of Paul who was originally from Lystra. My soldiers led the prisoners down to Herod the Great's marvel, the Caesarea Harbor; a man-made breakwater boarded on the north, west, and south by barriers constructed of lime and volcanic ash; a wondrous feat by any standard. Here we boarded a ship heading for the province of Asia.

It became quite obvious to me that Paul was no criminal. He was rather a man dedicated to one he called Messiah; one, he claimed, who was sent by the Jewish god to help both Jews and Gentiles. The first night on board was quiet. We arrived at Sidon. Paul asked that he might be allowed to visit his friends in the city. I saw no reason to object, "Paul, you may visit your friends and take your companions with you. I will provide what help you need. My only rule: guards must accompany you at all times." Paul agreed.

The next day was windy; a south westerly wind. It forced us to sail under the protection of the north side of the island called Cyprus, sailing near Cilicia and Pamphylia and reaching Myra in Lycia on the southern coast of Asia. Here we found a grain ship sailing for Rome. I arranged passage on it.

Forward progress was slow; the winds were against us. It was with difficulty that we reached Cnidus, a safe Asian port. A northwest wind raging down the Aegean Sea prevented us from continuing west, so on the ship captain's order we headed southwest toward Crete, passing the east end of the island around Cape Salmone until we arrived at a place called Safe Harbors. The ship's captain ordered, "We will stay here until the wind changes."

There was considerable personal interaction during this wait. I got to know Paul rather well. He shared his faith with me and with others. There was no question; this man was driven; driven by an unstoppable determination to share his message about this Jesus of Nazareth who Paul claimed was raised from death. Forgiveness of sin was an important part of his message. That importance became apparent to us, when one day, while sailing, Paul asked that I permit him and his friends to honor the following day by fasting and holding a private prayer time aboard ship. He explained that it was important to him because of what would take place in the Jerusalem Temple the next day. He said, "Tomorrow is a most holy day for all Jews. It is the tenth of the month Tishrei; the day of *Yom Kippur* – Day of Atonement."

I thought, "What an interesting request." I said, "Tell me, Paul, what is this *Yom Kippur*? Explain it. I would like to know more of your religion. It fascinates me." As best as I can remember, this was his explanation:

"If I and my companions were in Jerusalem tomorrow, we would be celebrating *Yom Kippur*, one of the holiest days of the year for those who follow the Jewish tradition. It is a time when Jews fast and pray; when they promise to be better people; when the High Priest performs acts symbolizing Yahweh forgiving sins. The whole day is devoted to forgiveness of sin."

Paul continued, "There is much pageantry. The service begins as the High Priest, stepping into a special *mikvah*, a washing pool located in the Temple's Court of Gentiles, washes himself with particular focus to his hands and feet. He then, wearing golden garments, performs the regular morning offering. Following another washing, the High Priest changes into a linen garment. He now sacrifices a bull as his personal sin-offering. The congregation responds with prayer. The next act involves two goats held outside the Court of Israel. One is selected by lot "for the Lord" and one for *Azazel*, the "devil." The next step is physically difficult. It requires that the High Priest transport a shovel full of hot embers from the Altar while also carrying a vessel containing incense. Both are carried into the Holy of Holies, enclosing the room with sweet smelling smoke. Next, some of the blood collected from the sacrificed bull is carried to the Holy of Holies and sprinkled about; the vessel is then set in the Holy Place.

"Focus now centers back to the two goats. The High Priest walks to the Nicanor Gate, lays his hands on the goat "for the Lord," and pronounces a confession on behalf of the priests. The congregation responds with prayer. The goat is then carried to the Altar and slaughtered; its blood collected in a vessel and some of it sprinkled in the Holy of Holies. The vessel is then set in the Holy Place. Levites now carry both vessels to the Holy Altar and pour the contents together. The remaining blood of the goat and the bull is first painted on the four corners of the Altar, then sprinkled on the Altar.

"Next, the High Priest lays his hands on the goat for *Azazel* and makes a general confession for the entire population of Israel. The congregation responds with prayer. He then sends the goat off to a cliff just outside Jerusalem where it is pushed over the edge, symbolizing that all sins for all Israel are forever removed.

"Following readings from the Torah, there is more washing, burning, and changing of garments. All is finalized, when wearing a linen garment, the High Priest removes the bowl of incense and the shovel from the Holy Place. A new washing with change into another golden garment and two more washings of hands and feet complete the ritual. There is a total of five immersion baths and ten ritual washing of hands."

My only response was, "Wow!"

✣ ✣ ✣

While Paul's story was an interesting diversion, it did not resolve our problem, the weather. While still in Safe Harbors, Paul insisted that we must not sail; it was too late in the fall; conditions could make sailing very dangerous. He warned, "I know these waters well. I've sailed them many times. Men, I see that our voyage from here on will be dangerous; there will be great damage to the cargo and to the ship; and loss of life as well." The captain argued, "I also know these waters. I've sailed them in late fall and I've had rough weather, but I've always made it through. Our ship is large. It can handle rough seas. We will sail – if the weather improves. – This harbor is not a desirable winter stop-over. We will be better served if we go on to Phoenix. It's a good place to spend the winter. We will be able to enjoy the camaraderie of other sailors *held-up* for the winter." All looked at me. Since this grain ship was licensed by

Rome, I held the highest rank aboard. I had the power to make the final decision. I ordered, "I judge that the captain's advice is most dependable. We will sail – if – if the weather becomes favorable. The ship's crew agreed.

A soft wind from the south was our signal to raise sail. We again cruised westward, as close to the mainland of southern Crete as possible. But soon a very strong wind – the one called "Northeaster" – what the sailors called a *Euraquilo* – blew with violence down from the island's seven thousand foot mountains. Our ship was rocked by the waves and pushed away from the island. The captain tried to steer the ship back to the coast, but the force of the gale made it impossible; the ship would not move forward in that direction. The captain gave orders to let the ship be carried along by the wind. We were thrown to-and-fro, moving westward without control. Luckily we found some shelter when we passed very near to and south of the little island of Cauda. The waves lessened briefly, giving the crew time to secure the ship's life boat by pulling it aboard. Ropes were used to undergird the ship, strengthening it against the waves.

There was fear that the winds against the sails would carry us farther south, causing us to run aground on sand bars off the coast of Libya. All sails were lowered and tied. The ship was turned into the wind. It would follow the winds and currents of the sea; moving westerly and away from the African coast.

There seemed no end; the violent storm continued. For many days we could see neither sun nor stars. The captain ordered that cargo and all heavy equipment be thrown overboard. I did not dare show it, but I was convinced that we would all die. The men became hysteric; they refused food.

It was about this time that my prisoner, Paul took control. He shouted to the crew, "Men, you should have listened to me and not have sailed from Crete; then we would have avoided all this damage and loss. But now I beg you, take courage! Not one of you will lose his life; only the ship will be lost. For last night an angel of the God to whom I belong and whom I worship came to me and said, 'Don't be afraid, Paul! You must stand before the Emperor, and God in his goodness has given you the lives of all those who are sailing with you.' And so, men, take courage! For I trust in God that it will be just as I was told. But we will be driven ashore on some island."

✠ ✠ ✠

About midnight on the fourteenth night the sailors suspected that we were getting close to land. They dropped a line with a weight tied to it and found that the water was one hundred and twenty feet deep; a little later they did the same and found that it was ninety feet deep. Four anchors were quickly dropped to assure we would not dash into a rocky coast. Paul led the men in prayer; men who were fearful but trusting.

As soon as the prayers ended, Paul approached me with a warning. "Commander Julius, some sailors are at this moment lowering the ship's life boat into the water. Timothy heard their conversation earlier. These men are pretending to follow orders; orders not given. They have told crew members that they were ordered to lower the boat into the water and use it to untie the anchors located on the sides and to the front of our ship. This is a ruse; they intend to ride the boat to shore; deserting us. If these sailors don't stay on board, you cannot be saved."

I ordered, "Stop these men! Cut the ropes and release the boat!" It was done. As we approached daylight, Paul called the crew together, "Men, eat some food. You have been waiting for fourteen days now, and all this time you have not eaten. I beg you, then, eat some food; you need it in order to survive.

I promise you, not even a hair of your heads will be lost" He then took some bread, gave thanks to his God, broke it, and began to eat. I could see a change in the men; there was a confidence. There were smiles. Every one of them took food and ate; all two hundred and seventy-six.

St. Paul's ship wreck

When all had finished, work began. The captain ordered the wheat stored below to be cast into the sea. After about three hours, the captain gave the command to stop. There was a noticeably lessened sea displacement. We were definitely riding higher in the water.

☩ ☩ ☩

No one recognized the coast. We did see a bay with a beach. The captain ordered all anchor ropes cut, the ropes holding the two steering oars cut, and the front sail raised. He would try to guide the boat into the bay. The wind blew the ship forward and headed for shore, but the ship hit a sandbank and went aground; the front part of the ship stuck solidly in the mud and clay below. Everything stopped; then a shudder. The back of the ship began to heave; it was breaking apart. Waves hammered against the rear; pieces broke loose; water burst into the hold.

My soldiers responded with terror! They panicked! "Kill the prisoners! If they escape we will suffer! We will be held responsible! Kill the prisoners!" But that didn't happen. I surged to the front of my troop. "Attention! Attention, I said! Fall in! You cannot kill the prisoners. You cannot kill Paul. He's your friend! He's a man of God! I order you to abandon ship! Abandon ship, now! If you can swim, jump into the water and swim to shore. If you cannot swim, grab some lumber and hang on to it as you paddle to shore. Save yourselves and save the prisoners!" – Everyone made it safely to shore. It was a miracle; – none was lost.

Several island locals were watching as the waves battered our ship. We jumped; we swam; we clutched onto timbers; we paddled. The locals called encouragement. They entered the water; supporting us as we urged our bodies closer to shore, in some cases dragging men who were about to give up; so beaten and exhausted were they. Men shivered from exposure as they lay on the sand. Then it started to rain, and it was cold. A fire was built and the men huddled around it. Those able gathered wood. Paul gathered a bundle of sticks and as he put them on the fire a poisonous snake slithered out and fastened his teeth on Paul's hand. I heard a shout, "This man must be a murderer, but Fate will not let him live, even though he escaped from the sea!" Paul shook the snake off his hand. We waited for it to swell up. We expected him to fall dead from the poison. We waited . . . and waited. Nothing happened. Then another shout, "This man is a god! Neither the sea nor the snake's poison can harm him. He is a god!"

Word of the wreck and Paul's miracle healing reached a man named Publius. He was the chief of this island, Malta. A servant approached and invited all of us to his home. Accommodations were found among his servants' and among neighboring housing. We were all treated kindly; stayed for three days as his personal guests. Time spent proved to be a blessing for Publius. His father was in bed, sick with fever and dysentery. Paul prayed, placed his hands on him, and healed him. Nothing was the same after that. Sick men and women from all over the island came to Paul for healing. The result, we were showered with gifts; treated like royalty.

Paul sails for Rome: Acts 27:1-28:10

Then Paul Said

I am Paul; a Pharisee, missionary, teacher, preacher, miracle worker, guest of Publius, and prisoner of Caesar. The three months we spent on Malta were both energizing and spiritually uplifting. I truly learned to appreciate the goodness of Yahweh; how he had blessed me with a power beyond my expectations. There were healings daily. My host was genuinely kind and generous. As you might imagine, the citizens treated me as if I were a god. In fact, it was sometimes difficult to convince the populace that I was not a god, but rather a servant of the one and only most high God.

A ship whose figurehead was the twin gods, Castor and Pollux, berthed among those harbored on the island. Since it was carrying grain to Puteoli, Julius arranged that we board it to complete our voyage to Rome. We set sail. After a three day stay in Syracuse, we sailed on to Rhegium, and since a favorable south wind was blowing, set off for our final port, Puteoli. Can you imagine my joy when we were greeted by a small congregation of believers? They had heard from passengers on an earlier ship that we were coming. We were asked to stay with them. I approached Julius. I knew he would try to accommodate my request; he had become a believer. Most of his crew and most of the prisoners had become believers. He did and we stayed. I needed this intermission; soon I would be in Rome facing that mad emperor, Nero. Anything could happen.

As we continued north toward Rome we approached the market of Appius and Three Inns. Once more God showed his kindness. We were met by brothers, men who had heard of our presence on the mainland and came to greet and comfort us. God be thanked!

I will be ever thankful to Julius. Because of his friendship I was not placed into a prison, but rather allowed to live in a house. My only restriction: Under most circumstances I must be chained to a Roman guard. I could not have asked for more.

I sent out a call to meet with the Jewish leadership of Rome. After three days some local Jewish leaders came to my house. After showing proper introductory etiquette, I clarified my situation. "My brothers – even though I did nothing against our people or the customs that we received from our ancestors, I was made a prisoner in Jerusalem and handed over to the Romans. They questioned me and wanted to release me, because they found that I had done nothing for which I deserved to die. But when the Jews opposed this, I was forced to appeal to the Emperor, even though I had no accusation to make against my own people. That is why I asked to see you and talk with you; because I have this chain on me for the sake of him for whom the people of Israel hope."

The men talked among themselves, then the one I assumed of highest position spoke, "We have not received any letters from Judea about you, nor have any of our brothers come from there with any news, or to say anything negative about you. But we would like to hear your ideas, because we know that everywhere people speak against this party that you belong to." Following more casual conversation, we agreed to set a date for a formal meeting in which I would explain what these men regarded as a new version of Judaism.

✠ ✠ ✠

It was a long day. From morning till night I explained and gave the men the message of the Kingdom of God. I tried to convince them about Jesus by quoting from the Law of Moses and the writings of the prophets. Some were convinced by my words; others would not believe. There was obvious disagreement within the group. I warned, "How well the Holy Spirit spoke through the prophet Isaiah to your ancestors! For he said:

> *Go and say to this people:*
> *You will listen and listen, but not understand;*
> *You will look and look, but not see.*
> *Because this people's minds are dull,*
> *They have stopped up their ears,*
> *And have closed their eyes.*
> *Otherwise, their eyes would see,*
> *Their ears would hear;*
> *Their minds would understand,*
> *And they would turn to me, says God,*
> *And I would heal them.'"*

I concluded with this declaration, "You are to know, then, that God's message of salvation has been sent to the Gentiles. They will listen!"

✠ ✠ ✠

My house arrest did not last long. I was brought to trial. Nero did not preside. The only accusation against me was the letter written by Governor Festus. It spoke of charges brought by the Jewish priests claiming that I had defiled the Temple and had spoken openly against Jewish Law. Since there were no other allegations against me, Rome had no interest in what they considered the Jew's religion peculiarities and the case was quickly dismissed. I was a free man. I and my trusty companions rented a house in Rome. Daily visits brought men and women of faith to our dwelling – and I was able to *walk-the-streets* – to speak publicly and freely about the Kingdom of God and the Lord Jesus Christ. My stay as a free man in Rome lasted for two years. – I chose to leave, there was still more work to do.

I was compelled to again share the Good News with fellow Jews and Gentiles outside of Rome. Luke, Timothy, Titus, and I took our leave of Rome and sailed to Crete. During our brief previous visit, while being taken as a prisoner to Rome, I was able to briefly meet with some who were of the faith. I intended that this visit also be short. Our plan was to have Titus stay on Crete to establish the budding churches and appoint elders. Luke, Timothy, and I then sailed to Israel and visited with James the Just and those disciples still living there.

After a restful return to Antioch, Syria, it was agreed that Luke would remain, while Timothy and I would begin another tour. We re-visited congregations in Asia, traveling through Cilicia and reaching Colossae in Phrygia. With the help of brothers I was able to send a letter to Titus, asking him to spend the winter with me in Nicopolis. We stopped at Ephesus. There were problems that needed attention. Since it proved necessary that someone I could trust remain behind to establish order and government in the church, I left Timothy there with a direct command to the elders that, even though he is young, they respect his spiritual leadership. Erastus joined me. Our journeys took us first to Miletus where we found a ship for Troas. After sharing time with the brothers, we crossed over to

Nicopolis and on to Philippi, Thessalonica, Berea, and Corinth. It was good to be with our Corinthian brothers; we had been through a lot together. But my plans were to spend the winter in Nicopolis. I was able to arrange that a letter be sent to Titus inviting him to spend the winter with me. Erastus chose to stay in Corinth.

My friend and companion Luke now lived in Nicopolis. "What joy! We were together again!" Titus arrived shortly after me. We spent profitable months together; Luke and me as teachers; Titus as student.

✠ ✠ ✠

It was my desire to bring the Good News to Spain. The option became reality following our stay in Nicopolis. A ship was sailing as far west as the Pillars of Hercules. This was my chance. As soon as the seas were safe, the ship sailed. My wish would be granted; I would visit Spain. – The product of my fifteen month stay: birth of vibrant new churches. As summer ended I left Spain and sailed eastward with stops at Corinth and Miletus, ending in Troas. It was here where it became obvious that the end of my earthly life was nearing.

Earlier, during our brief stop in Corinth we heard reports that there had been a devastating fire in the city of Rome. We were told that a third of the city had been destroyed. Rumors as to its cause were rampant and many. That was all we knew.

The port of Miletus was alive with threatening reports. "It was the Christians! They started it! These blood drinkers burned our capital city!" I cautiously entered the port city to inquire about my friend Trophimus who became sick at my last visit to Miletus and was left with the brothers. His health had returned. Soon we were off to Troas, and then hopefully, after a short stop, to Nicopolis.

There was a Jewish posse waiting as we disembarked at Troas; vigilantes who were set on killing anyone Christian. They regarded the events in Rome a perfect opportunity to eradicate the evil that had fallen upon Judaism. I was spotted immediately. "Grab him! Grab that man! That man is Paul, a leader of these blasphemers!" I was mobbed; wrestled to the ground and beaten. I would have died, except a squad of Roman soldiers came to the rescue. The sergeant in charge demanded an explanation. "He is a Christian! He is a leader of those who burned Rome! He deserves to die!" A circle of spears encircled the sergeant and me; pointing outward. The mob backed away. The sergeant asked, "They call you Paul. Who are you? What have you done?" My immediate response, "I am Christian, a Jew, and I am a Roman citizen born in Tarsus, capital of the province of Cilicia."

"Why do these men want to kill you, a citizen of Rome? – I repeat, what have you done?" "I am a leader of those who are called Christians. We believe and teach that Jesus of Nazareth was put to death on a cross in Jerusalem and three days later rose from death. We believe he is the Messiah; the son of God."

The sergeant yelled to the mob, "Who will speak for you Jews? A priest shouted back, "I will! What this Paul preaches is punishable by death. He teaches that Jesus of Nazareth is the Messiah, the King of the Jews. Only Caesar Nero can be honored as king. He must so be revered by all. Hail Caesar!" The sergeant appeared impressed. He threatened, "Were you not a citizen of Rome, I would let the mob have you and be rid of you. But since you are a citizen, I must bring you before a tribunal for judgment. Your fate will rest in their hands."

Guards ushered me to a prison; a dark, damp hole. My only light: a barred window high above my head. My only companions: three rats, each hoping to compete with me for the gruel and water pushed through the door twice each day. I think it was day seven when the cell door opened and I was led into a judgment hall to stand before three magistrates. The charges ended with the words: "The man before you regards a Jew, Jesus of Nazareth, as his king and teaches this treason to both Jews and Gentiles. Such treachery cannot be tolerated. He must die!"

I was asked to speak – knowing what would happen if convicted: death. "I have committed no crime. It is true; I am a Christian. That is my only offense. I hold allegiance to Nero as my earthly king, but Jesus of Nazareth is my spiritual king. He is the son of the most high God, Yahweh. I am innocent of treason. I am a loyal Roman citizen. Unless this court is willing to declare me innocent, I appeal that my case be brought before Caesar!" After a short consultation the ruling was pronounced. "You appealed to Caesar, to Caesar you will go."

My second boat ride to Rome witnessed calm seas but rat infested cells, deep within the hold. Walking in chains from the port city of Puteoli to Rome caused excruciating pain to my ankles. Skin was raw and flesh infected. We finally arrived at my prison home. Because I was considered special, a Roman citizen who had appealed to Caesar, I was placed into a cell by myself. I thought how circumstances had changed. Last time, a leisure walk with friends from Puteoli to Rome instead of this chain-bound march. Last time, an in-house arrest instead of this cell. Last time, an earth-life future instead of this anticipated heaven-life future.

St. Paul led as prisoner to Rome

This was for me, a time to reflect God's mercy. During the almost thirty years of travel that reached to the ends of the empire, I talked with thousands of people, and wrote many letters to churches and individuals. In each encounter I tried to help my brothers and sisters walk the path set before them by our God.

✠ ✠ ✠

Among my first letters were messages I wrote from Corinth to the church in Thessalonica. Many thought Jesus would return during their lifetimes. I learned from Timothy about concerns for those who had already died, before his expected return. Their question, "What happens to these people?" I assured them that those who died before Christ's return would be raised from death and those still living would be changed. In a second letter I wrote about the Lord's return as judge.

While in Ephesus, I receive information of problems in Corinth. So I, together with my brother Sosthenes, wrote a letter to guide them back into spiritual harmony. There were divisions among the saints that needed resolution. We also responded to a variety of questions. I dealt with concerns related to tongues and prophesying, the resurrection, women and the church, and the centrality of love.

Following the riot in Ephesus I left and traveled to Macedonia. Titus was there to meet me. He told about a crisis that had developed. There were some in the Corinthian congregation who challenged my legitimacy as an apostle of Christ. I quickly wrote a second letter carried by Titus, intending it to reach Corinth prior to my arrival. I addressed their concern. I wrote regarding life after death. I offered directives and encouragement regarding the collection for the church in Jerusalem. I concluded with a definition and defense of my ministry as an apostle; including a description of my rapture into heaven.

While on my third journey I responded to concerns among some Galatian Christians; concerns related to the Law of Moses. Since many in the congregation were Jews or were influenced by them, the question, "Must I obey the Laws of Moses?" became a major issue. There were those I called Judaizers who insisted that Christians must come to God through Judaism. While I did not encourage my fellow Jews to ignore the Law, I did make it clear that obedience to the Law could not be used as the path to God, and that to insist Gentiles must subject themselves to the demands of the Law was false teaching. All that God requires is: faith in Jesus; – belief that his suffering, death, and resurrection are all God requires. My message was: You are saved by grace, through faith in Christ, and not by the submission to the Law.

St. Paul writing his epistles

While in Corinth and before I was able to travel to Rome, it became necessary that I write to Christians there. I learned that they also were bothered by an insistence of some that since the Mosaic Law is an expression of the will of God, it is a universal obligation to live according to it mandates. My message was the same as to the Galatians: Because of our sinful nature we cannot live up to the Law's standards. But Christ has kept the Law for us; he suffered and died to pay the penalty of all sin; he rose from death as assurance that his sacrifice satisfied the judgment of God. Therefore, allegiance is not to the Law, but rather to Jesus whose intervention overcame the Law. My friend Phoebe carried this letter.

While in prison, I wrote four letters. My letter to the Ephesians focused on unity of the Church. I feared that the Church might split into two churches: A Jewish Christian Church and a Gentile Christian Church. I encouraged oneness, a universality of believers. I believed that Christ accepted all believers, including those of different races, viewpoints, and prejudices. The letter concluded with a series advising how to live the righteous life.

In my letter to the Philippians, what some called my missionary letter, I emphasized the true joy that comes from Jesus Christ alone. I wrote on the themes of humility, self-sacrifice, unity, and of course, expressed my profound thanks for the gift of money that Epaphroditus carried from Philippi.

To the Colossians, I presented Christ as God in the flesh, Lord of all creation, and the head of the Church. I also addressed the problem of false teachers promoting a "higher thought" cult, a form of legalism.

A short letter was addressed to my friend, Philemon. One of his slaves, Onesimus, had stolen some of his master's property and run away. During his time of fleeting freedom he became a Christian and my friend. I told Onesimus that he had to return to his master. I then wrote Philemon to accept his former slave as a brother rather than slave. I hoped by this letter to encourage believers everywhere to treat others with Christian love and fellowship.

Letters were also sent to my young pastors, Timothy and Titus. I encouraged Titus to direct his Cretan congregation to exemplary behavior. While in Macedonia I sent my first letter to Timothy. I guided the young minister in his role as spiritual leader. My second letter was written later, during my second imprisonment in Rome; a product of the Neronian Persecution. It was Nero who maliciously announced that the catastrophic burning of Rome was caused by Christians. They were totally innocent. But because of Nero's lie, I was taken prisoner; taken to Rome. It was a bad time. I felt abandoned. I was sure that death was near. I assured Timothy of the rightness of our ministry; even though persecution was the rule of the land; even though the faithful were being martyred, some by wild beasts. My message was: "We must continue to teach and live our faith; even in the face of death. God will overcome. His kingdom will never end. It will be triumphant."

I have done my best in the race. I have run the full distance, I have kept the faith. And now the prize of victor is waiting for me, the crown of righteousness which the Lord, the righteous Judge, will give me on that Day – and not only to me, but to all those who wait with love for him to appear.

The end of my earthly life is near. I will be martyred; because I am a Roman citizen, not by crucifixion, but beheaded. Soon I will be in heaven with my God. There is no better future. Praise Him! – Come Lord Jesus.

Paul in Rome: Acts 28:11-31
Titus remains in Crete: Titus 1:5
Paul winters in Nicopolis: Titus 3:12
Paul plans to go to Spain: Romans 15:24, 28
Timothy remains in Ephesus: 1Timothy 1:3
Paul plans to revisit Macedonia: Philippians 2:24
Paul's final plea: 2 Timothy 4:7-8

Let us give thanks to the God and father of our Lord Jesus Christ! For he has blessed us, in our union with Christ, by giving us every spiritual gift in the heavenly world. Before the world was made, God had already chosen us to be his in Christ, so that we would be holy and without fault before him. Because of his love, God had already decided that through Jesus Christ he would bring us to himself as his sons – this was his pleasure and purpose. Let us praise God for his glorious grace, for the free gift he gave us in his dear Son!

For by the death of Christ we are set free, that is, our sins are forgiven. How great is the grace of God, which he gave to us in such large measure! In all his wisdom and insight God did what he had purposed, and made known to us the secret plan he had already decided to complete by means of Christ. God's plan, which he will complete when the time is right, is to bring all creation together, everything in heaven and on earth, with Christ as the head.

All things are done according to God's plan and decision; and God chose us to be his own people in union with Christ because of his own purpose, based on what he had decided from the very beginning. Let us, then, who were the first to hope in Christ, praise God's glory! Ephesians 1:3-12

END OF BOOK FIVE

Appendix A –

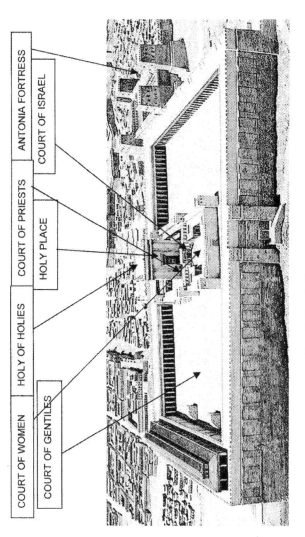

COURT OF WOMEN

COURT OF GENTILES

HOLY OF HOLIES

COURT OF PRIESTS

HOLY PLACE

ANTONIA FORTRESS

COURT OF ISRAEL

Herod's Temple Mount

http://en.wikipedia.org/wiki/File:Jerusalem_Modell_BW_2.JPG

Herod's Temple Mount

Appendix B –

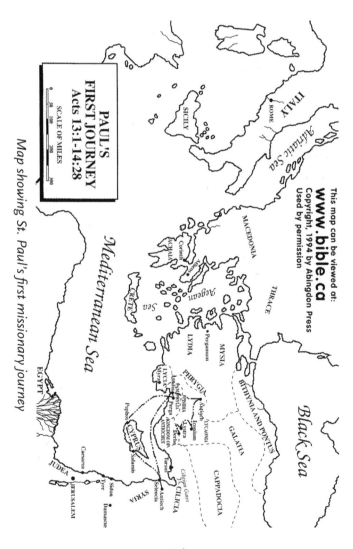

Map showing St. Paul's first missionary journey

124

Appendix C –

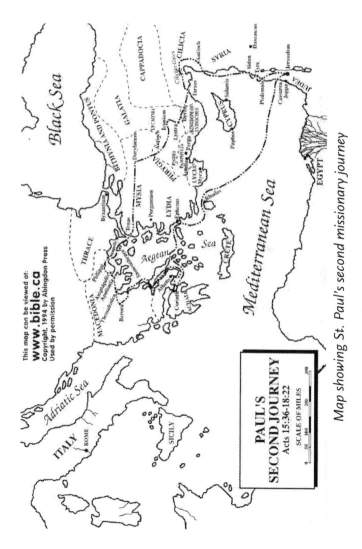

Map showing St. Paul's second missionary journey

Appendix D –

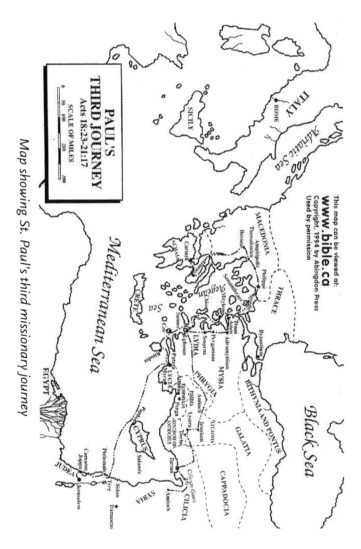

Map showing St. Paul's third missionary journey

126

Appendix E –

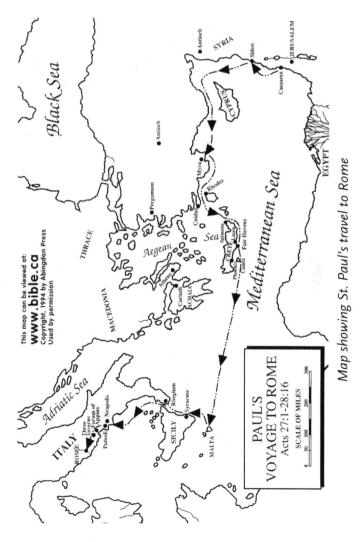

Map showing St. Paul's travel to Rome

127

Discussion Questions

You may wish to use *Narratives of St. Paul's Missionary Journeys and Rome* for Youth or Adult Bible Discussion. Below are questions that may be helpful.

*Please note: Some of the questions refer to content that is based on non-Biblical sources and/or is the author's creation. Such narrative has no certain truth of Scripture at its base. Answers attributed to such content are identified with asterisks * and should be understood as coming from an historical novel and not historical truth.*

Then Mark Said –

Mark: 14:51-52; Luke 12:12
Cyprus ministry: Acts 13:1-13

1. Who were Mark, Mary, and Barnabas?
2. Other than Jerusalem, which city was a major center of Christianity?
3. How did the Antioch church make decisions?
4. Why was Cyprus a logical first outreach attempt?
5. *Why did Lazarus move from Bethany to Kition?
6. Who was Elymas? How was he discredited?
7. What action of Paul led Sergius Paulas to become a believer?

8. *Why did Paul and Barnabas choose to travel to Pisidian Antioch?
9. Had you been part of Paul's missionary group, would you have risked crossing the Taurus Mountains?
10. If you had written *Then Mark Said* how would the content of the story differ?

Then Pomona Said –
Pisidian Antioch: Acts 13:14-52

1. *What persuaded Lucius and Pomona to invite Paul and Barnabas to find room and board at their home?
2. What was the substance of Paul's Sabbath message?
3. *What did some Jews fear would happen?
4. Why did Paul and Barnabas leave the city?
5. If you had written *Then Pomona Said* how would the content of the story differ?

Then Timothy Said –
Antioch in Pisidia, Lystra, Derbe/Return to Antioch in Syria: Acts 14:1-28
Standards for the church: 1Timothy 3:2-4

1. Who are Eunice, Lois, Timothy, and Timothy's father?
2. What miracle did Paul perform?
3. What was the crowd's reaction?
4. Why the connections: Paul as Hermes and Barnabas as Zues?
5. *What happened to cause Paul to be stoned? What ended the stoning?
6. What places were visited after leaving Lystra and returning to Antioch, Syria?
7. If you had written *Then Timothy Said* how would the content of the story differ?

Then James the Just Said –

The Jerusalem Council meets: Acts 15:1-35
James' quotation: Amos: 9:11-12
Laws of Moses: Exodus 34:15-17; Leviticus 18:6-23; 17:10-16

1. *Who is James the Just? What do you know of him?
2. What divisive issue confronted the Church in Antioch, Syria?
3. *How wide spread was this issue?
4. How would you have judged, had you been part of the Council?
5. List at least two arguments for limiting Gentile submission to the Law?
6. What was the final judgment of the Council?
7. If you had written *Then James the Just Said* how would the content of the story differ?

Then Paul Said –

Beginning of the second journey: Acts 15:36-16:5
God's secret: Ephesians 3:6-7

1. *Who is young Paul?
2. Detail events that led Paul to become a messenger for Jesus?
3. *Describe the argument related to John Mark's future role as missionary.
4. Where did Barnabas and Mark minister?
5. Where in Asia did Paul and Silas minister?"
6. Describe events that led to Timothy joining Paul and Silas?
7. Had you been Timothy's parent, would you have let him go?
8. If you had written *Then Paul Said* how would the content of the story differ?

Then Luke Said –
From Troas to Philippi: Acts 16:6-40

1. Who is Luke?
2. *During what parts of Paul's life were he and Paul together?
3. Where did the Philippi Jews come together for worship?
4. What was the response to Paul's sermon?
5. What is the distinction awarded Lydia?
6. *What forced Paul to exorcize the evil spirit from the slave girl?
7. What was the result of this action?
8. Describe what happened at midnight?
9. What must a person do to be saved?
10. What did Paul require of the local Roman officials?
11. *What did Luke do?
12. If you had written *Then Luke Said* how would the content of the story differ?

Then Paul Said –
Paul in Thessalonica, Berea, and Athens: 17:1-34

1. *What happened to Jason and other Christians? Why?
2. What about Athens impressed Paul?
3. What is generous about Paul's Areopagus sermon?
4. Were any brought to faith?
5. If you had written *Then Paul Said* how would the content of the story differ?

Then Priscilla Said –

Paul in Corinth: Acts 18:1-23
Nazarite vow: Numbers 6:1-21

1. Who are Priscilla and Aquila? What is their history?
2. How did Paul spend his first weeks in Corinth?
3. *What was the tramway? Why was it important to Corinth?
4. Who is Gallio?
5. What was the accusation against Paul?
6. What was the verdict?
7. Why was this verdict important?
8. What happened to Sosthenes?
9. What are the demands of a Nazarite vow?
10. Who was Erastus? How did he help the missionary effort?
11. If you had written *The Priscilla Said* how would the content of the story differ?

Then Apollos Said –

Apollos: Acts 18:24-19:10

1. *Who is Apollos? Describe his history.
2. What instruction did Aquila and Priscilla offer Apollos?
3. To where did Apollos go after leaving Ephesus?
4. If you had written *Then Apollos Said* how would the content of the story differ?

Then Demetrius Said –

Paul in Ephesus: Acts 19:11-41

1. *What was Artemis?
2. Why was Paul a threat to Demetrius and other craftsmen?

3. What happened when the sons of Sceva tried to exorcize and evil spirit?
4. Describe the events that brought a mob into the theater.
5. How was the matter resolved?
6. If you had written *Then Demetrius Said* how would the content of the story differ?

Then Silas Said –
Review of the 2nd and 3rd journeys: Acts 15-19
Returning to Jerusalem: Acts 20:1-21:16

1. When did Silas begin a friendship with Paul?
2. How many cities can you name that were evangelized by Paul?
3. If you had written *Then Silas Said* how would the content of the story differ?

Then Michael Said –
Paul's visit to Jerusalem: Acts 21:17-23:24
Temple sacrifices: Leviticus 1, 2, 3, 4
Rules for a Nazarite: Numbers 6:1-21

1. *What was the relationship between Paul and his family? Why?
2. Does such persecution happen in today's world? Describe.
3. *Who was Michael?
4. Shortly after Paul arrived in Jerusalem, what did the brothers ask Paul to do?
5. *Why did Paul first complete a Rite of Purification?
6. Describe the Nazarite Rite of Absolution.
7. *What happened after the conclusion of the Rite of Absolution?
8. What was the zealot plan?

9. Summarize Paul's defense on the steps of the Antonio Fortress.
10. What defense strategy did Paul use before the Council?
11. How did Michael help save Paul's life?
12. How did the commander assure Paul's safety?
13. If you had written *Then Michael Said* how would the content of the story differ?

Then Governor Felix Said –

Paul before Governor Felix: Acts 23:25-24:27

1. Who is Felix? Drusilla?
2. What was the essence of Tertullus' accusation?
3. What was Paul's defense before Felix?
4. *Why did Felix refuse to release Paul?
5. If you had written *Then Governor Felix Said* how would the content of the story differ?

Then Governor Festus Said –

Paul before Festus and Agrippa: Acts 25:1-26:32

1. Who is Festus? *What appears to be the reason he replaced Felix?
2. Why did Festus keep Paul imprisoned?
3. What was Paul's appeal?
4. *Who are Herod Agrippa II and Bernice?
5. Why could Paul speak more directly to Agrippa rather than he could to Festus?
6. How was God's hand applied in this part of Paul's life?
7. If you had written *Then Governor Festus Said* how would the content of the story differ?

Then Julius Said –

Paul sails for Rome: Acts 27:1-28:10

1. *Who was Julius?
2. What is *Yom Kippur*?
3. What actions focused on forgiveness for the High Priest?
4. Describe the actions associated with the two goats.
5. What actions focused on forgiveness for the Temple priests?
6. What action focused on forgiveness for the whole of Israel?
7. Had you been at Safe Harbors with Paul, would you have voted to sail for Phoenix?
8. For how many days was the ship carried by the storm?
9. Describe the drama once land was sighted.
10. How did God direct Paul's actions while on the island of Malta?
11. If you had written *Then Julius Said* how would the content of the story differ?

Then Paul Said –

Paul in Rome: Acts 28:11-31
Titus remains in Crete: Titus 1:5
Paul winters in Nicopolis: Titus 3:12
Paul plans to go to Spain: Romans 15:24, 28
Timothy remains in Ephesus: 1Timothy 1:3
Paul plans to revisit Macedonia: Philippians 2:24
Paul's final plea: 2 Timothy 4:7-8

1. Describe Paul's journey from Malta to Rome.
2. What was the result of Roman Jews visiting Paul while he was a prisoner?
3. *Why was Paul exonerated by the Roman court?

4. List places Paul may have visited after becoming a free man?
5. Why were Christians being persecuted?
6. *How did Paul die?
7. For each of Paul's letters:
   From where was it written?
   What was its focus?